POOLEYS FLIGHT GUIDE

NORTH-WEST FRANCE

FEBF

GW00722768

R(
William Ryan

Asst. Editors
Roy Patel
Sharon Copsey

ISBN
0 902037 31 5

TO PAT

POOLEYS FLIGHT GUIDES LIMITED,
ELSTREE AIRPORT, HERTS., WD6 3AW
TEL: 081-953-4870. FAX: 081 953 5219

Intentionally Blank

CONTENTS

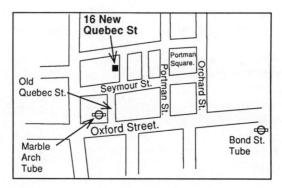

INTRODUCTION

General
The information contained in this Flight Guide Supplement is intended for use in connection with visual flight operations only. Although details are given for Runway Approach and Aerodrome Let-Down facilities, these should not be used in IMC without reference to the appropriate Let-Down Procedure Chart.

Aerodrome Coverage
Full details are given of all general aviation aerodromes in North-West France, along with brief details of restricted aerodromes and military aerodromes. The large international airports are not included.

Note.
It is regretted that it is not possible to provide an amendment service for this publication.

IMPORTANT

This Flight Guide is not an official aeronautical information publication and should be used as a guide only. Reference should always be made to the relevant A.I.P. and NOTAMs. The information in this Guide has been compiled from official sources and is considered to be as reliable as possible. While great care has been exercised in the compilation of this Guide the editors and publishers will not be held responsible for any inaccuracies or omissions therein.

R. J. Pooley
W. J. Ryall

LOW LEVEL CROSS-CHANNEL OPERATIONS
BETWEEN THE UNITED KINGDOM AND FRANCE

The required procedures for flights wishing to cross the English Channel between the United Kingdom and France are as follows:

Flight Planning
Pilots undertaking Cross-Channel flights are reminded that a flight plan MUST be filed for all flights to or from the United Kingdom which will cross the United Kingdom/France FIR boundary.

When filing the flight plan with the UK and French Authorities, pilots are to ensure that well defined significant points/features, at which the aircraft will cross the UK and French coastlines, are included in Item 15 (Route) of the flight plan form (eg Beachy Head, Berck sur Mer, Lydd, Boulogne, Dover, Cap Gris Nez, etc). This is mainly for Search and Rescue purposes but will also assist ATC.

Pilots should plan their flights, where possible, at such altitudes which would enable radio contact to be maintained with the appropriate ATC Unit whilst the aircraft is transitting the Channel. In addition, the French Authorities have requested that aircraft fly at altitudes which will keep them within radar cover. The carriage of Secondary Surveillance Radar (SSR) equipment is recommended.

Position reports are required when crossing the coast outbound, inbound and when crossing the FIR boundary.

IFR Operations
Pilots undertaking Cross-Channel flights under IFR are reminded that normal IFR Rules apply particularly regarding altitudes and flight levels. Pilots are also reminded that the IMC rating is **not** recognised by the French Authorities.

General Information
The London Air Traffic Control Centre (LATCC) at West Drayton provides a flight information service to pilots flying in the open FIR. The service for the area in question is available on frequency 124·600 with the call sign 'London Information'. It is emphasised that the FIS is only informatory. The FIR controller cannot:

- Exercise positive control over aircraft; or
- issue clearance to alter course, climb or descend; or
- give positive advice on the avoidance of collision.

The Royal Air Force, also at West Drayton, provide a 24 hour nationwide emergency cover for both civil and military aircraft from the Distress and Diversion Section (D and D) at that Unit. The Distress and Diversion controllers can, in the event of an emergency, select from a wide range of radio and radar facilities which provide cover over the whole of the United Kingdom and surrounding sea areas. In addition to the services currently available, West Drayton is expected to introduce a new computerised aircraft position fixing service, provided specifically for civil light aircraft pilots, early in 1993.

Pilots are reminded that the emergency service is available on frequency 121·500 and in addition, to indicate an emergency condition, SSR Transponder Code 7700 should be selected, except that if the aircraft is already transmitting a code and receiving an air traffic service that code will normally be retained.

When entering United Kingdom airspace from an adjacent region where the operation of transponders has not been required, pilots of suitably equipped aircraft should select Code 2000.

Mode C should be operated with the above codes.

There is also a Lower Airspace Radar Service (LARS) unit at RAF Manston which can provide a service to a limited number of aircraft.

CROSS-CHANNEL CONTROLLING AUTHORITIES
AND FLIGHT INFORMATION SERVICE (FIS)

London FIS...........................London Information 124·60
FIS ....Manston App 126·35 (LARS)
FIS ....Lydd App 120·70
Calais TMA ....Calais App 122·70
Le Touquet TMA...................Le Touquet App 125·30
Paris (North) FIS ....Paris Info 125·70

FRENCH AIRSPACE
RULES & REGULATIONS

FLIGHT PLANS

A flight plan may be submitted:
- as a filed flight plan before flight or, during flight when necessitated by unforseen circumstances or;
- during flight for the purpose of transmitting flight data to an ATS unit.

A flight plan is mandatory for:
- **All IFR flights;**

- **VFR flights crossing the borders of Metropolitan France** — Border crossing point must be indicated under ITEM 10 of the flight plan form and under ITEM 18 giving ETA at border crossing. The flight plan must be submitted 30 minutes before estimated departure from the apron;

- **VFR flights over Maritime Regions** — When the distance from the coast exceeds the lower of the following two distances:
    (a) the distance required to ensure that a landing can be made on land in the event of engine failure;
    (b) a distance equivalent to 15 times the altitude of the aircraft;

- **Night VFR flights** — flight plan must be filed at least 30 minutes before estimated take-of time or, if submitted during flight, 30 minutes before sunset at destination aerodrome.

Airborne Flight Plan
An 'abbreviated flight plan' may be filed **in the air** before entering class 'D' controlled airspace, traffic circuits of controlled aerodromes or before operating under Special VFR. Unless otherwise prescribed by the appropriate ATS authority, the closure of the abbreviated flight plan shall be made either in person on landing or by radio on leaving the controlled airspace.

Closing a Flight Plan
If the arrival aerodrome is equipped with an ATS unit (TWR or AFIS), the radio communication exchange on landing is sufficient to close the flight plan.

When no ATS unit exists at the arrival aerodrome, the arrival report must be made as soon as possible after landing by the quickest means available to the nearest ATS unit.

A flight plan may be closed by radio a few minutes before landing by communicating with an ATS unit.

Flight Information Centre Telephone Numbers:

Bordeaux	56 47 95 01
Brest	98 44 79 63
Marseille	42 33 76 76
Paris	69 84 51 03
Reims	26 05 03 08

CLASSIFICATION OF FRENCH AIRSPACE

Class 'A', 'D', 'E' and 'G' are implemented in France as follows.
- FIR up to FL115 (or 3,000' SFC whichever is higher):
  outside controlled airspace: Class 'G';
  within controlled airspace: Class 'A', 'D' or 'E' according to airspace and activity.
- FIR from FL 115 (or 3,000' SFC whichever is higher) up to FL195: Class 'D'.
- At and above FL195: Class 'A'.

ATS AIRSPACE CLASSIFICATIONS and VMC MINIMA

Airspace	Separation	Services	VMC Minima	Speed Limit	Radio	ATC Clearance
Class A (IFR)	All aircraft	ATC service	Not applicable	N/A	Required	Required
(VFR)	Not Permitted					
Class B	Not Allocated					
Class C	Not Allocated					
Class D (IFR)	IFR/IFR	Traffic information IFR/VFR (Traffic avoidance advice on request)	Not applicable	N/A	Required	Required
(VFR)	Not provided	Traffic information VFR/IFR and VFR/VFR flights. (Traffic avoidance advice on request)	Vis 8 km, 1500 m and 1000 ft from cloud.	N/A	Required	Required
Class E (IFR)	IFR/IFR	ATC service and traffic information about VFR traffic as far practical.	Not applicable	N/A	Required	Required
(VFR)	Not provided	Traffic information as far as practical	Vis 8 km, 1500 m and 1000 ft from cloud.	N/A	Not required	Not required
Class F	Not Allocated					
Class G (IFR)	Not provided	Flight information service.	Not applicable	N/A	Not required	Not required
(VFR)	Not provided	Flight information service	Vis 8 km, 1500 m and 1000 ft from cloud.		Not required	Not required

VFR Landing/Take-Off Minima

Except when a Special VFR clearance has been obtained from ATC, VFR flights shall not take-off or land from/at an aerodrome within a CTR or enter the traffic circuit when conditions are less than surface visibility 8 km, ceiling 1500 ft.

Minimum Overflight Heights

General Rule

Except for take-off and landing and related procedures, aircraft must fly at levels that are above or equal to the highest of the following levels:
The minimum level imposed by the Visual Flight Rules which are defined as follows:
(a) the minimum height which would permit the aircraft, when flying over towns and other built up areas, to alight clear and without danger to persons or property in the event of a power failure;
(b) minimum heights that may be set by decree dated 10 October 1957, relative to the overflying of towns and other built-up areas, the overflying of gatherings of people or animals in open areas and the overflying of certain sites or buildings.

Minimum VFR Level

In addition to compliance with the above general rule, except for take-off and landing procedures and related manoeuvers, no VFR flight may be undertaken:
(a) over high density areas, towns or other built-up areas, or over gatherings of people in open areas, at less than 1,000 ft above the highest obstacle located within a radius of 600 m of the aircraft;

(b) in areas other than those mentioned in (a), at a height of less than 500 ft above ground or water and at a distance of less than 150 m from any person, vehicle or ship on the surface or from any artificial obstacle.

Preferential Utilization of Low Altitude Airspace
Military low level operations are mostly carried out Monday to Friday between SR plus 30 minutes and SS minus 30 minutes. These operations are conducted at very high speed below 1500' SFC:

(a) Within restricted areas when, due to the nature of the operation, military pilots are not always able to apply the 'see and avoid' rule. It is therefore imperative that pilots operating under VFR comply strictly with the requirement to obtain entry clearance.

(b) outside restricted airspace and over French territory, below 1500' SFC with visibility generally better than 5 km.

Pilots operating under VFR are recommended to:

• conduct their flights at a cruising level at or above 1500' SFC consistent with meteorological conditions and airspace restrictions;

• execute the minimum necessary manoeuvers below 1500' SFC during take-off and landing.

VFR Cruising Levels
VFR flights are required to fly at the following cruising levels when operating above 3000' amsl or 1000' SFC (whichever higher).

Mag Track 000° – 179°: Flight Levels 35, 55, 75, and 95

Mag Track 180° – 359°: Flight Levels 45, 65, 85 and 105.

Special VFR Minima
The SVFR minima varies to some extent with different aerodromes. The applicable SVFR minima for a particular aerodrome is given under the appropriate aerodrome entry in the following pages.

Transponders
Transponders (mode A or C) are mandatory:

• within Class D Airspace (mode C recommended);

• above FL120 or 2,000' SFC (whichever is higher).

Intentionally Blank

LFAB ....Dieppe (St Aubin)		LFCE*......Guéret (St.-Laurent)
LFAC ....Calais-Dunkirk		LFCF*......Figeac (Livernon)
LFAD ....Compiègne (Margny)		LFCG*......St-Girons (Antichan)
LFAE ....Eu (Mers-le-Tréport)		LFCH.......Arcachon (La Teste de Buch)
LFAF*......Laon (Chambry)		LFCI ....Albi (Le Sequestre)
LFAG ....Péronne (St-Quentin)		LFCJ........Jonzac (Neulles)
LFAI*.......Nangis (Les Loges)		LFCK*......Castres (Mazamet)
LFAJ*.......Argentan		LFCL ....Toulouse (Lasbordes)
LFAK*......Dunkirk (Ghyvelde)		LFCM ......Millau (Larzac)
LFAL*......La Fleche (Thorée-les-Pins)		LFCN*.....Nogaro
LFAM* .....Berck-sur-Mer		LFCO*.....Oloron (Herrère)
LFAN*......Condé-sur-Noireau		LFCP*......Pons (Avy)
LFAO*......Bagnoles-de-l'Orne (Couterne)		LFCQ*......Graulhet (Montdragon)
LFAP*......Rethel (Perthes)		LFCR.......Rodez (Marcillac)
LFAO ....Albert (Bray)		LFCS ....Bordeaux (Léognan-Saucats)
LFAR*......Montdidier		LFCT*......Thouars
LFAS*......Falaise (Monts d'Eraines)		LFCU* .....Ussel (Thalamy)
LFAT ....Le Touquet (Paris-Plage)		LFCV*......Villefranche-de-Rouergue
LFAU*......Vauville		LFCW*.....Villeneuve-sur-Lot
LFAV........Valenciennes (Denain)		LFCX*......Castelsarrasin (Moissac)
LFAW* .....Villerupt		LFCY ....Royan (Médis)
LFAX*......Mortagne-au-Perche		LFCZ*......Mimizan
LFAY........Amiens (Glisy)		LFDA*......Aire-sur-l'Adour
LFBA ....Agen (La Garenne)		LFDB*......Montauban
LFBB ....Bordeaux FIC (ACC/UAC)		LFDC* .....Montendre (Marcillac)
LFBC ....Cazaux		LFDE*......Egletons
LFBD ....Bordeaux (Mérignac)		LFDF*......Sainte-Foy-La-Grande
LFBE ....Bergerac (Roumanière)		LFDG*......Gaillac (Lisle-sur-Tarn)
LFBF ....Toulouse (Francazal)		LFDH.......Auch (Lamothe)
LFBG.......Cognac (Châteaubernard)		LFDI*.......Libourne (Artigues de Lussac)
LFBH.......La Rochelle (Laleu)		LFDJ* ......Pamiers (Les Pujols)
LFBI........Poitiers (Biard)		LFDK*......Soulac-sur-Mer
LFBJ* ......St. Junien		LFDL* ......Loudun
LFBK.......Montluçon-Guéret		LFDM*......Marmande (Virazeil)
LFBL........Limoges (Bellegarde)		LFDN*......Rochefort (St.-Agnant)
LFBM.......Mont-de-Marsan		LFDO.......Bordeaux (Souge)
LFBN.......Niort (Souché)		LFDP*......St-Pierre d'Oléron
LFBO.......Toulouse (Blagnac)		LFDQ* .....Castelnau-Magnoac
LFBP ....Pau (Pyrénées)		LFDR* .....La Réole (Floudés)
LFBQ.......ENAC - Toulouse		LFDS*......Sarlat (Domme)
LFBR.......Muret (Lherm)		LFDT*......Tarbes (Laloubére)
LFBS*......Biscarrosse (Parentis)		LFDU* .....Lesparre (St-Laurent-Médoc)
LFBT ....Tarbes (Ossun-Lourdes)		LFDV*......Couhé (Vérac)
LFBU.......Angoulème (Brie-Champniers)		LFDW*.....Chauvigny
LFBV ....Brive (La Roche)		LFDX*......Fumel (Montayral)
LFBW ......Mont-de-Marsan (CCT)		LFDY*......Bordeaux (Yvrac)
LFBX.......Périgueux (Bassillac)		LFEA*......Belle-Ile
LFBY ....Dax (Seyresse)		LFEB*......Dinan (Trélivan)
LFBZ ....Biarritz-Bayonne (Anglet)		LFEC*......Ouessant
LFCA*......Châtellerault (Targe)		LFED*......Pontivy
LFCB*......Bagnères-de-Luchon		LFEE ....Reims FIC/ACC/UAC
LFCC.......Cahors (Lalbenque)		LFEF*......Amboise (Dierre)
LFCD* .....Andernos-les-Bains		LFEG* .....Argenton-sur-Creuse

* Not on AFTN circuit

LFEH*......Aubigny-sur-Nére	LFGK*.....Joigny
LFEI*......Briare (Châtillon)	LFGL*.....Lons-le-Saunier (Courlaoux)
LFEJ*......Châteauroux (Villers)	LFGM*....Montceau-les-Mines (Pouilloux)
LFEK*......Issoudun (Le Fay)	LFGN*.....Paray-le-Monial
LFEL*......Le Blanc	LFGO*.....Pont-sur-Yonne
LFEM*.....Montargis (Vimory)	LFGP*.....St-Florentin (Chéu)
LFEN*.....Tours (Sorigny)	LFGQ*.....Semur-en-Auxois
LFEP*.....Pouilly (Maconge)	LFGR*.....Doncourt-les-Conflans
LFEQ......Quiberon	LFGS*.....Longuyon (Villette)
LFER*.....Redon (Bains-sur-Oust)	LFGT*.....Sarrebourg (Buhl)
LFES*.....Guiscriff (Scaer)	LFGU*.....Sarreguemines (Neunkirch)
LFET*......Til-Châtel	LFGV*.....Thionville (Yutz)
LFEU*......Bar-le-Duc (Les Hauts de Chee)	LFGW*....Verdun (Rozelier)
LFEV*.....Gray (St.-Adrien)	LFGX*.....Champagnole (Crotenay)
LFEW*....Saulieu (Liernais)	LFGY*.....St. Dié (Rémomeix)
LFEX*.....Nancy (Azelot)	LFGZ*.....Nuits-St-Georges
LFEY.......Ile d'Yeu (Le Grand Phare)	LFHA*......Issoire (Le Broc)
LFEZ*.....Nancy (Malzéville)	LFHC*.....Pérouges (Meximieux)
LFFA ....PARIS FIC (ACC/UAC/NOF)	LFHD*.....Pierrelatte
LFFB*......Buno-Bonnevaux	LFHE*.....Romans (St-Paul)
LFFC*.....Mantes (Chérence)	LFHF*.....Ruoms
LFFD*......St -André-de l'Eure	LFHG*.....St. Chamond (L'Horme)
LFFE*......Enghien (Moisselles)	LFHH*.....Vienne (Reventin)
LFFF ....Paris FIC (ACC/UAC/NOF)	LFHI*......Morestel
LFFG*......La Ferté-Gaucher	LFHJ*......Lyon (Corbas)
LFFH*.....Château-Thierry (Belleau)	LFHK*.....Camp de Canjuers
LFFI ....Ancenis	LFHL*......Langogne (Lespéron)
LFFJ*......Joinville (Mussey)	LFHM......Megève
LFFK*......Fontenay-le-Comte	LFHN*.....Bellegarde (Vouvray)
LFFL*......Bailleau-Armenonville	LFHO......Aubenas (Vals-Lanas)
LFFM*......Lamotte-Beuvron	LFHP......Le Puy (Loudes)
LFFN*......Brienne-le-Château	LFHQ......St. Flour (Coltines)
LFFP*......Pithiviers	LFHR*.....Brioude (Beaumont)
LFFQ*.....La Ferté-Alais	LFHS*.....Bourg (Ceyzériat)
LFFR*.....Bar-sur-Seine	LFHT*.....Ambert (Le Poyet)
LFFS*......Suippes (MET OBS)	LFHU......L'Alpe d'Huez
LFFT ....Neufchâteau (Rouceux)	LFHV.......Villefranche (Tarare)
LFFU*.....Châteauneuf-sur-Cher	LFHW*....Belleville (Villié-Morgon)
LFFV*......Vierzon (Méreau)	LFHX*.....Lapalisse (Périgny)
LFFW*....Montaigu (St-Georges)	LFHY*.....Moulins (Montbeugny)
LFFX*......Tournus (Cuisery)	LFHZ*.....Sallanches (Mont-Blanc)
LFFY*......Etrépagny	LFIB*......Belvès (St-Pardoux)
LFFZ*......Sézanne (St-Rémy)	LFIC ....Cross Corsen
LFGA ......Colmar (Houssen)	LFID*......Condom (Valence-sur-Baise)
LFGB*.....Mulhouse (Habsheim)	LFIE ....Cross Etel
LFGC*.....Strasbourg (Neuhof)	LFIF*........St. Affrique (Belmont)
LFGD*......Arbois	LFIG*......Cassagnes-Begonhès
LFGE*......Avallon	LFIH*.......Chalais
LFGF*.....Beaune (Challanges)	LFIJ.........Cross Jobourg
LFGG*.....Belfort (Chaux)	LFIK*.......Ribérac (St -Aulaye)
LFGH*.....Cosne-sur-Loire	LFIL*.......Rion-des-Landes
LFGI*......Dijon (Darois)	LFIM*......St-Gaudens (Montréjeau)
LFGJ ....Dole (Tavaux)	LFIN ....Cross Gris-Nez

* Not on AFTN circuit

Pooley's Flight Guides ©

LFIP*......Peyresourde (Balestas)	LFMC......Le Luc (Le Cannet)
LFIR*.......Revel (Montgey)	LFMD......Cannes (Mandelieu)
LFIT*.......Toulouse (Bourg-St-Bernard)	LFME ......Nimes (Courbessac)
LFIV*......Vendays-Montalivet	LFMF ......Fayence
LFIX*......Itxassou	LFMG* ....La Montagne Noire
LFIY*.......St-Jean-d'Angely	LFMH ......St. Etienne (Bouthéon)
LFJG ....Cross La Garde	LFMI........Istres (Le Tubé)
LFJL........Metz (Nancy Lorraine)	LFMJ ....Nice/Mont Agel (CCT)
LFKA* .....Albertville	LFMK ......Carcassonne (Salvaza)
LFKB ......Bastia (Poretta)	LFML.......Marseille (Marignane)
LFKC......Calvi (Ste Catherine)	LFMM......Aix-en-Provence
LFKD* ....Sollières-Sardières	(MARSEILLE FIC/ACC/UAC/COM)
LFKE* .....St-Jean-en-Royans	LFMN ......Nice (Côte d'Azur)
LFKF ....Figari (Sud Corse)	LFMO ......Orange (Caritat)
LFKG* .....Ghisonaccia (Alzitone)	LFMP ......Perpignan (Rivesaltes)
LFKH* .....St. Jean-d'Avelanne	LFMQ ......Le Castellet
LFKJ ....Ajaccio (Campo dell'Oro)	LFMR*.....Barcelonnette (St.-Pons)
LFKL*......Lyon (Brindas)	LFMS ......Alès (Deaux)
LFKM* .....St. Galmier	LFMT ......Montpellier (Fréjorgues)
LFKO.......Propriano (Tavaria)	LFMU ......Béziers (Vias)
LFKP* .....La Tour du Pin (Cessieu)	LFMV ......Avignon (Caumont)
LFKS ....Solenzara	LFMW ......Castelnaudary (Villeneuve)
LFKT*......Corte	LFMX ......Château-Arnoux (St.-Auban)
LFKY* .....Belley (Peyrieu)	LFMY ......Salon
LFKZ*.....St. Claude (Pratz)	LFMZ* ....Lézignan-Corbières
LFLA ....Auxerre (Branches)	LFNA.......Gap (Taliard)
LFLB ......Chambery (Aix-les-Bains)	LFNB.......Mende (Brénoux)
LFLC ....Clermont-Ferrand (Aulnat)	LFNC* .....Mont-Dauphin (St.-Crépin)
LFLD ......Bourges	LFND* .....Pont-St-Esprit
LFLE*......Chambéry (Challes-les-Eaux)	LFNE.......Salon (Eyguières)
LFLF ....Orléans (COM)	LFNF* .....Vinon
LFLG.......Grenoble (Le Versoud)	LFNG ......Montpellier (Candillargues)
LFLH ....Chalon (Champforgeuil)	LFNH* .....Carpentras
LFLI........Annemasse	LFNI*.......Conqueyrac
LFLJ.......Courchevel	LFNJ*......Aspres-sur-Buech
LFLK*......Oyonnax (Arbent)	LFNK* .....Vars (Les Crosses et Les Tronches)
LFLL........Lyon (Satolas)	LFNL*......St. Martin-de-Londres
LFLM......Macon (Charnay)	LFNM......La Mole
LFLN ......St. Yan	LFNO* .....Florac (Sainte-Enimie)
LFLO ......Roanne (Renaison)	LFNP* .....Pézenas (Nizas)
LFLP ....Annecy (Meythet)	LFNQ* .....Mont-Louis (La Quillane)
LFLQ.......Montélimar (Ancône)	LFNR* .....Berre (La Fare)
LFLR*......St.-Rambert d'Albon	LFNS* .....Sisteron (Thèze)
LFLS ....Grenoble (St.-Geoirs)	LFNT* .....Avignon (Pujaut)
LFLT ....Montluçon (Domérat)	LFNU* .....Uzès
LFLU ....Valence (Chabeuil)	LFNV* .....Valréas (Visan)
LFLV........Vichy (Charmeil)	LFNW* ....Puivert
LFLW......Aurillac	LFNX* .....Bédarieux (La Tour-sur-Orb)
LFLX ....Châteauroux (Déols)	LFNY* .....St. Etienne-en-Dévoluy
LFLY.......Lyon (Bron)	LFNZ* .....Le Mazet de Romanin
LFLZ* ......Feurs (Chambéon)	LFOA.......Avord
LFMA ......Aix (Les Milles)	LFOB ......Beauvais (Tille)
LFMB ......Aix-en-Provence (4ème Region AIR)	LFOC ......Châteaudun

* Not on AFTN circuit

LFOD ......Saumur (St-Florent)	LFQE ......Etain (Rouvres)
LFOE ......Evreux (Fauville)	LFQF* .....Autun (Bellevue)
LFOF* .....Alençon (Valframbert)	LFQG ......Nevers (Fourchambault)
LFOG*.....Flers (St-Paul)	LFQH* .....Châtillon-sur-Seine
LFOH ......Le Havre (Octeville)	LFQI ....Cambrai (Epinoy)
LFOI* ......Abbeville	LFQJ ....Maubeuge (Elesmes)
LFOJ ....Orléans (Bricy)	LFQK* .....Chalons (Ecury-sur-Coole)
LFOK ......Chalons (Vatry)	LFQL* .....Lens (Bénifontaine)
LFOL* .....L'Aigle (St-Michel)	LFQM* ....Besancon (La Vèze)
LFOM* ....Lessay	LFQN* .....St. Omer (Wizermes)
LFON* .....Dreux (Vernouillet)	LFQO ......Lille (Marq-en-Baroeul)
LFOO ......Les Sables d'Olonne (Talmont)	LFQP ......Phalsbourg (Bourscheid)
LFOP ......Rouen (Boos)	LFQQ ......Lille (Lesquin)
LFOQ*.....Blois (Le Breuil)	LFQR* .....Romilly-sur-Seine
LFOR* .....Chartres (Champhol)	LFQS* .....Vitry-en-Artois
LFOS* .....St. Valéry (Vittefleur)	LFQT.......Merville (Calonne)
LFOT ....Tours (St. Symphorien)	LFQU* .....Sarre-Union
LFOU ......Cholet (Le Pontreau)	LFQV ......Charleville-Mézières
LFOV.......Laval (Entrammes)	LFQW* ....Vesoul (Frotey)
LFOW* ....St. Quentin (Roupy)	LFQX* .....Juvancourt
LFOX* .....Etampes (Mondésir)	LFQY* .....Saverne (Steinbourg)
LFOY* .....Le Havre (St.-Romain)	LFQZ* .....Dieuze (Guéblange)
LFOZ* .....Orléans (St.-Denis de l'Hôtel)	LFRA.......Angers (Avrillé)
LFPA ....Persan-Beaumont	LFRB.......Brest (Guipavas)
LFPB ....Paris (Le Bourget)	LFRC ......Cherbourg (Maupertus)
LFPC.......Creil	LFRD ....Dinard (Pleurtuit/St.-Malo)
LFPD* .....Bernay (St.-Martin)	LFRE ....La Baule-Escoublac
LFPE ....Meaux (Esbly)	LFRF ....Granville
LFPF* ......Beynes (Thiverval)	LFRG ......Deauville (St.-Gatien)
LFPG ......Paris (Charles-de-Gaulle)	LFRH ......Lorient (Lann-Bihoué)
LFPH.......Chelles (Le Pin)	LFRI ....La Roche-sur-Yon (Les Ajoncs)
LFPI ....Paris (Issy-les-Moulineaux)	LFRJ ....Landivisiau
LFPJ ....Taverny	LFRK.......Caen (Carpiquet)
LFPK.......Coulommiers (Voisins)	LFRL.......Lanveoc (Poulmic)
LFPL ....Lognes (Emerainville)	LFRM ......Le Mans (Arnage)
LFPM ......Melun (Villaroche)	LFRN ......Rennes (St.-Jacques)
LFPN.......Toussus-le-Noble	LFRO ......Lannion
LFPO ......Paris (Orly)	LFRP* .....Ploermel (Loyat)
LFPP* .....Le Plessis-Belleville	LFRQ ......Quimper (Pluguffan)
LFPQ* .....Fontenay-Trésigny	LFRR ....Brest FIC/ACC/UAC/CCT
LFPR.......Guyancourt	LFRS.......Nantes (Atlantique)
LFPS.......Paris (Town/Ville)	LFRT.......St.-Brieuc (Armor)
LFPT ....Pontoise (Cormeilles-en-Vexin)	LFRU.......Morlàix (Ploulean)
LFPU* .....Moret (Episy)	LFRV.......Vannes (Meucon)
LFPV.......Villacoublay (Vélizy)	LFRW* ....Avranches (Le Val St.-Père)
LFPW ......Toulouse (MET Centre)	LFRX.......Brest (Préfecture Maritime)
LFPX.......Chavenay (Villepreux)	LFRY.......Cherbourg (Préfecture Maritime)
LFPY.......Bretigny-sur-Orge	LFRZ.......St. Nazaire (Montoir)
LFPZ.......St. Cyr-l'Ecole	LFSA* .....Besancon (Thise)
LFQA* .....Reims (Prunay)	LFSB.......Bâle-Mulhouse
LFQB ......Troyes (Barberey)	LFSC.......Coimar (Meyenheim)
LFQC*.....Luneville (Croismare)	LFSD.......Dijon (Longvic)
LFQD* .....Arras (Roclincourt)	LFSE* .....Epinal (Dogneville)

* Not on AFTN circuit

LFSF.......Metz (Frescaty)	LFXW......Camp du Larzac
LFSG......Epinal (Mirecourt)	LFYA.......Drachenbronn (CCT)
LFSH*.....Haguenau	LFYD*....Damblain
LFSI........St. Dizier (Robinson)	LFYF.......Centre Météorologique de
LFSJ*.....Sedan (Douzy)	Concentration et de Diffusion FAF
LFSK*.....Vitry-le-Francois (Vauclerc)	LFYG*.....Cambrai (Niergnies)
LFSL.......Toul (Rosières)	LFYH*.....Broye-les-Pesmes
LFSM*.....Montbéliard (Courcelles)	LFYL.......Lure (Malbouhans)
LFSN.......Nancy (Essey)	LFYM......Marigny-le-Grand
LFSO......Nancy (Ochey)	LFYO.......Villacoublay (Centre OPS COTAM)
LFSP.......Pontarlier	LFYR.......Romorantin (Pruniers)
LFSQ......Belfort (Fontaine)	LFYS.......Sainte-Léocadie
LFSR.......Reims (Champagne)	LFYT.......St. Simon (Clastres)
LFST.......Strasbourg (Entzheim)	LFYX.......Paris (Etat Major AIR)
LFSU*.....Langres-Rolampont	LFZZ Collective SNOWTAN address
LFSV*.....Pont-St-Vincent	
LFSW*....Epernay (Plivot)	LNMC......Monaco
LFSX.......Luxeuil (St-Sauveur)	
LFSY*.....Chaumont (La Vendue)	
LFSZ*......Vittel (Champ~de Courses)	
LFTB.......Marignane (Berre)	
LFTC.......Toulon (Contrôle)	
LFTF.......Cuers (Pierrefeu)	
LFTH.......Hyères (Le Palyvestre)	
LFTN*.....La Grand' Combe	
LFTP.......Puimoisson	
LFTR.......Toulon (St-Mandrier)	
LFTS......Toulon (Préfecture Maritime)	
LFTU.......Fréjus (St-Raphaël)	
LFTW......Nîmes (Garons)	
LFWB......S.C.C.O.M. South West	
LFXA.......Ambérieu	
LFXB*.....Saintes (Thénac)	
LFXC......Contrexeville (CCT)	
LFXD.......Doullens/Lucheux (CCT)	
LFXE.......Camp de Mourmelon	
LFXF.......LimogeslRomanet	
LFXG......Camp de Bitche	
LFXH.......Camp du Valdahon	
LFXI........Apt/St. Christol	
LFXJ.......Bordeaux (3eme Région AIR)	
LFXK.......Camp de Suippes	
LFXL.......Mailly-le-Camp	
LFXM*.....Mourmelon	
LFXN.......Narbonne (CCT)	
LFXO......Tours/Cinq-Mars la Pile (CCT)	
LFXP.......Camp de Sissonne	
LFXQ......Camp de Coëtquidan	
LFXR.......Rochefort (Soubise)	
LFXS.......Camp de la Courtine	
LFXT.......Camp de Caylus	
LFXU.......Les Mureaux	
LFXV.......Lyon/Mont-Verdun	

* Not on AFTN circuit

Pooley's Flight Guides ©

LEGEND
AERODROMES

Aerodrome Features

Runway — Asphalt/Concrete/Bitumen

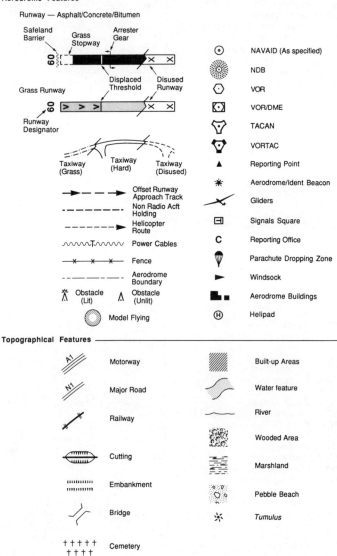

⊙	NAVAID (As specified)
	NDB
	VOR
	VOR/DME
	TACAN
	VORTAC
▲	Reporting Point
✳	Aerodrome/Ident Beacon
	Gliders
▱	Signals Square
C	Reporting Office
	Parachute Dropping Zone
►	Windsock
▪▪	Aerodrome Buildings
Ⓗ	Helipad

Safeland Barrier
Grass Stopway
Arrester Gear
Displaced Threshold
Disused Runway
Grass Runway
Runway Designator

Taxiway (Grass) Taxiway (Hard) Taxiway (Disused)

Offset Runway Approach Track
Non Radio Acft Holding
Helicopter Route
Power Cables
Fence
Aerodrome Boundary
Obstacle (Lit) Obstacle (Unlit)
Model Flying

Topographical Features

	Motorway		Built-up Areas
	Major Road		Water feature
	Railway		River
	Cutting		Wooded Area
	Embankment		Marshland
	Bridge		Pebble Beach
	Cemetery		*Tumulus*

16

LEGEND
VISUAL APP/DEP CHARTS

Aeronautical Information

Controlled Airspace

Compulsory Routes
(With Radio)

Class 'A' Airspace

Compulsory Routes
(Non Radio)

Class 'C' Airspace

VFR Routes
(Recommended)

Class 'D' Airspace

Transit Route

Class 'E' Airspace

Helicopter Route

FIR Boundary

Jet Aircraft Route

xxxxxxxxxxxxxxxx International Border

Danger/Restricted Area

Prohibited Area

Topographical Features

Runway(s)	Military Aerodrome	A1	Motorway
Holding Pattern	Civil Aerodrome	N1	Major Road
⊙	Private Airfield		Railway
NDB	Aerodrome/Ident Beacons		Bridge
⬡	Gliding		Built-up Areas
DME	Parachute Dropping Zone		Water feature
VOR/DME	Lighthouse		River
TACAN	Fort		Wooded Area
VORTAC	Windmill	Obstacle (Lit) Obstacle (Unlit)	
▲ Reporting Point (Advisory)		• Spot Height	
• Visual Reporting Point			

NORTH-WEST FRANCE
AREA OF COVERAGE
SHOWING
GENERAL AVIATION AERODROMES LISTED

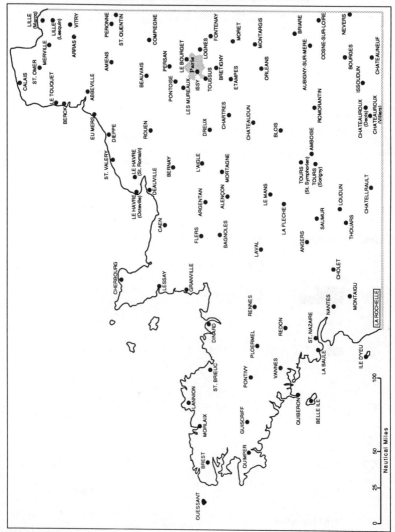

N5008·58 E00149·95	**ABBEVILLE**		220 ft AMSL

2·2nm NNE of Abbeville.   **BNE 113·80 190 29.   DPE 115·80 067 29**

MTD 113·65 330 45

No Radio.   FIS — Paris Information 125·70.
VOR 'ABB' 116·60 (298°/1nm to A/D)

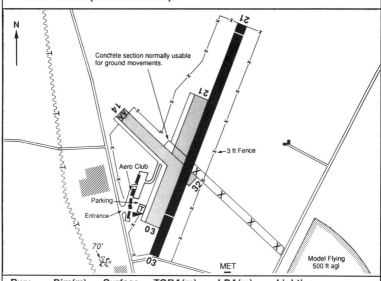

Rwy	Dim(m)	Surface	TORA(m)	LDA(m)	Lighting
03/21	1600x50	Concrete	03 -1600	03 -1340	Nil.
			21 -1600	21 -1550	Nil.
03/21	900x100	Grass	900	900	Nil.
14/32	635x80	Grass	14 -635	14 -605	Nil.
			32 -635	32 -635	Nil.

Op hrs: Sun-Fri 0820-1200 & 1400-1700 daily, Closed Sat.

Met: On A/D. Tel: 22 24 05 50   **AIS:** Beauvais (Tillé)

Customs: SR-SS 24hrs PNR preceding workday before 1700 hrs.

Restaurant: Available.   **Hangarage:** Available   **Maintenance:** Nil.

Remarks: Circuits LH on 03 & 32, RH on 21 & 14; powered aircraft at 1000 ft, gliders at 600 ft. Simultaneous use of Main Rwy 03/21 and parallel Grass Rwy prohibited. Glider operations from grass runways only. Aerodrome surface unusable outside Rwys & Twys. The NW end of disused concrete runway extends across Grass Rwy 03/21 without affecting ground movements. During periods of severe frost or after heavy rainfall exercise caution when using grass runways.

Fuel: 100LL.	**Tel:** 22 24 05 21 or 22 24 06 01 Aerodrome.
	22 24 08 48 Aero Club

LFOF

N4826·85 E00006·55	**ALENÇON (Valframbert)**	479 ft AMSL

1·3nm NNE of Alencon.   **LGL 115·00 225 27. CHW 115·20 271 36**

CAN 115·40 157 49

Auto Information 118·425. FIS — Paris Information 129·70.
Lctr 'AL' 380·0 (On A/D)

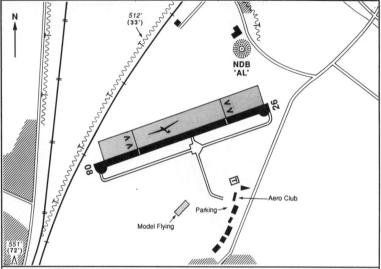

Rwy	Dim(m)	Surface	TORA(m)	LDA(m)	Lighting
08/26	775x18	Asphalt	08 -775	08 -565	Nil.
			26 -775	26 -595	Nil.
08/26	730x80	Grass	08 -730	08 -550	Nil.
			26 -730	26 -550	Nil.

Op hrs: On request SR-SS.

Met: On A/D. Tel: 33 29 26 96   **AIS:** Deauville (St. Gatien) Tel: 31 88 31 27

Customs: Nil.

Restaurant: Nil.   **Hangarage:** Available   **Maintenance:** Limited

Remarks: Circuits at 1000 ft., LH on 08, RH on 26. Glider/aerotowing activities on Grass Rwy 08/26.
Aerobatics area 2 nm NNE of airfield, 1650 – 3300 ft. agl. SR–SS.
Airfield unusable outside Rwys & Twys.
Mast 300 ft. agl 1·2 nm NNW of airfield.
Note. Danger Area LF-D507 3·75nm N of airfield.

Fuel: 100LL.	**Tel:** 33 29 25 86 Aerodrome (except Tues)

N4720·48 E00056·55	**AMBOISE (Dierre)**	180 ft AMSL

4·6 nm SSW of Amboise.	**AMB 113·70 227 06**
	POI 113·30 036 52

No Radio. Tours APP 121·00
FIS – Paris Information 129·62

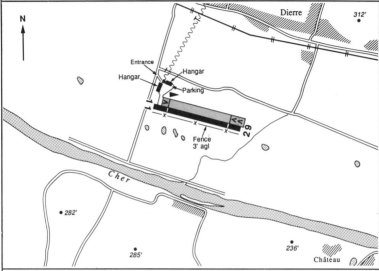

Rwy	Dim(m)	Surface	TORA(m)	LDA(m)	Lighting
11/29	700x25	Asphalt	11-700	11-555	Nil.
			29-700	29-615	Nil.
11/29	700x80	Grass	11-700	11-620	Nil.
			29-700	29-590	Nil.

Op hrs: On request. HJ

Met: Tours (St. Symphorien). 47 29 19 60. **AIS:** Tours (St. Symphorien). 47 54 02 81.

Customs: Nil.

Restaurant: Nil.	**Hangarage:** Nil.	**Maintenance:** Limited.

Remarks: Airfield situated beneath LF-R85C (3500' – FL55), activity status from Paris Information. Tours CTR 3·5 nm to the West, contact Tours App 121·00 — See TOURS Visual Approach/Dep Chart.
Circuits at 1000' to the south on Asphalt Rwy. Wide downwind leg required, to the south of RN 76 main road (approx 1 nm south of runway).
Gliders operate from Grass Rwy with circuits to the north at 1000'.
Simultaneous use of Asphalt Rwy and Grass Rwy prohibited.
Expect turbulence on approach to Rwy 29 when wind is south-westerly.
During calm or crosswind conditions use Rwy 11.
Aerobatic area to the south of Asphalt Rwy (1500' – FL35).
Airfield unusable outside Rwys and Twys.

Fuel: 100LL.	**Tel:** 47 57 93 91
0800-1200 & 1400-1800. Closed Tues.	

N4952·40 E00223·38	**AMIENS (Glisy)**	197 ft AMSL
3·7nm ESE of Amiens.	MTD 113·65 353 19.	BNE 113·80 161 49
	CMB 112·60 238 36.	ABB 116·60 130 27

Amiens Information 123·40 AFIS. FIS — Paris Information 125·70
Lctr 'GI' 339·0 (299°/3·9nm to Thr 30).

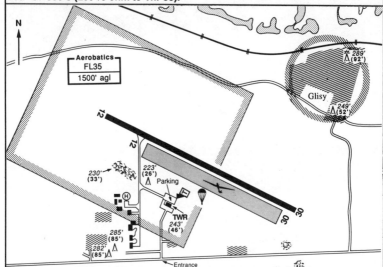

Rwy	Dim(m)	Surface	TORA(m)	LDA(m)	Lighting
12/30	1260x25	Asphalt	12 -1260	12 -1260	Thr Rwy
			30 -1260	30 -1260	Thr Rwy
12/30	900x100	Grass	12 -900	12 -900	Nil.
			30 -900	30 -900	Nil.

Op hrs: Mon-Fri 0900-1200 & 1400-1700. O/T PPR. Closed Sat, Sun & P. Hols.

Met: Abbeville. Tel. 22 24 50 50   **AIS:** Lille (Lesquin)

Customs: 6 hrs PNR. Mon-Fri 0800-1800. No attendance Sat & Sun.

Restaurant: Nil.   **Hangarage:** Available   **Maintenance:** Nil.

Remarks: Aerodrome situated beneath Paris TMA (Class **E**) base 3500' ALT.
Within the TMA contact Paris Control 128·275.
Circuit procedures: Asphalt Rwy — at 1000 ft; LH on 12, RH on 30.
Grass Rwy — at 700 ft; LH on 30, RH on 12.
Glider and microlight operations on Grass Rwy with circuits to South at 700 ft.
Simultaneous use of Asphalt and Grass Rwys is prohibited
Aerobatic Area 6070 at western end of airfield, 1500 ft. agl — FL35.
Airfield surface unusable outside Rwys & Twys.
Caution. Possible instrument approaches to Rwy 30.

Fuel: 100LL. (closed Mon)	**Tel:** 22 38 10 60 Aerodrome
	22 38 10 70 Aero Club

N4729·95 W00034·37	**ANGERS (Avrillé)**	187 ft AMSL
1·9nm NNW of Angers.	**ANG 113·00 105 12. NTS 115·50 067 47**	
	CLP 111·00 030 24	

Angers TWR 119·00.   FIS — Brest Information 122·80.
Lctr 'AS' 411·50 (129°/3·9nm to Thr 13).

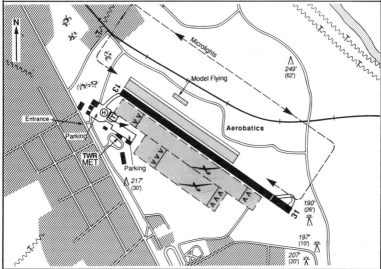

Rwy	Dim(m)	Surface	TORA(m)	LDA(m)	Lighting
13/31	1235x30	Asphalt	13 -1235	13 -1235	Thr Rwy
			31 -1235	31 -1100	Thr Rwy
13/31	800x60	Grass	13 - 800	13 - 800	Nil.
			31 - 800	31 - 800	Nil.

Op hrs: Mon-Fri (except PHs) 0800-1200 & 1400-1800.

Met: On A/D. Tel:41 34 32 19   **AIS:** Nantes Tel: 40 84 80 45

Customs: Mon-Fri 0800-2000(24 hrs PNR); Sat, Sun & PHs (O/R 24 hrs PNR)

Restaurant: Nil.   **Hangarage:** Nil.   **Maintenance:** Available

Remarks: Circuits at 700 ft aal; LH on 13, RH on 31. With wind less than 4 kt, use Rwy 31. Use of Asphalt Rwy 13/31 prohibited to non radio aircraft. Simultaneous use of parallel runways prohibited. Microlight activity on aerodrome. Glider operations (winch-launched) from grass strips on south side of main runway. Aerodrome surface unusable outside Rwys & Twys. Grass Rwys & Twys unusable after heavy rainfall. Possible instrument approaches to Rwy 13.
Aerobatic Area No.6355, 1300' SFC – FL35, at East end of airfield.
Take-off Rwy 13 — commence 90° turn to LEFT at 300 ft., but not before passing end of runway.
Take-off Rwy 31 — same procedure but turn RIGHT.
Avoid overflying factory 2 nm NW of aerodrome. **Caution:** Do not confuse Angers A/D with runway 13/31, 1500x12 m (not for public use) 3·2 nm to the NW.

Fuel: 100LL, Jet A1	**Tel:** 41 34 50 57 Twr. 41 34 42 85 Operator.
	Fax: 41 34 48 22 Twr. 41 88 09 04 Operator.

N4842·63 E00000·23	**ARGENTAN**	581 ft AMSL

2·2nm SSE of Argentan.	CAN 115·40 152 33
	CHW 115·20 293 41

No Radio.   FIS — Brest Information 122·80, Paris Information 129·62.

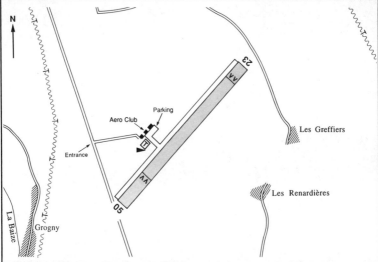

Rwy	Dim(m)	Surface	TORA(m)	LDA(m)	Lighting
05/23	1000x60	Grass	05 -1000	05 -800	Nil.
			23 -1000	23 -910	Nil.

Op hrs: PPR. SR–SS

Met: Rennes (St. Jacques).	**AIS:** Deauville (St. Gatien).

Customs: Nil.

Restaurant: Nil.	**Hangarage:** On request	**Maintenance:** Nil.

Remarks: Circuits left-hand at 1000 ft. With wind less than 4 kt, use Rwy 23.
Airfield surface unusable outside Rwys & Twys.

Fuel: 100LL (O/R preceding day from Aero Club. Cash)	**Tel:** 33 36 78 11 Aerodrome
	33 67 01 37 Aero Club

N5019·48 E00248·25	**ARRAS (Rolincourt)**	338 ft AMSL
2·1nm NE of Arras.	CMB 112·60 297 15. BNE 113·80 121 39	
	ABB 116·60 076 38	

No Radio.   FIS — Paris Information 125·70.

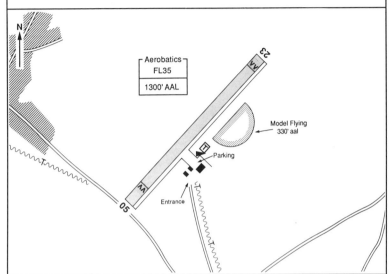

Rwy	Dim(m)	Surface	TORA(m)	LDA(m)	Lighting
05/23	1025x60	Grass	05 -1025	05 -895	Nil.
			23 -1025	23 -965	Nil.

Op hrs: PPR. SR–SS

Met: Lille (Villeneuve d'Ascq)	**AIS:** Lille (Lesquin).

Customs: Nil.

Restaurant: Nil.	**Hangarage:** On request	**Maintenance:** Nil.

Remarks: Circuits at 1000 ft; LH on 23, RH on 05.
Glider circuits at 700ft; LH on 05, RH on 23.
Aerobatic Area No.6020 on North side of runway, 1300 ft.aal — FL35.
Model flying on South side of runway, up to 330 ft. aal.
Take-off and landing prohibited when an aircraft is on the taxiway, between the displaced thresholds.
Airfield surface unusable outside Rwys & Twys. Possible restrictions after heavy rainfall or thawing; check with Paris Information.

Fuel: 100LL (available SR–SS except Tuesdays).	**Tel:** 21 55 36 74 Aerodrome
	21 21 21 41 Operator

Pooley's Flight Guides ©

LFEH

1·6 nm W of Aubigny-sur-Nère.   **NEV 113·40 315 29. BRG 110·40 012 28**
                                                           PTV 116·50 176 41

No Radio. FIS — Paris Information 126·10

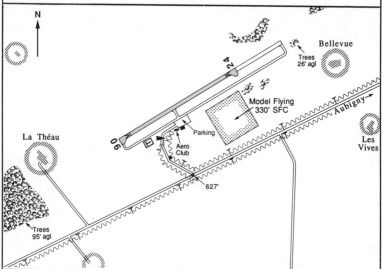

Rwy	Dim(m)	Surface	TORA(m)	LDA(m)	Lighting
06/24	1015x20	Grass	06-1000	06-925	Nil.
			24-1000	24-935	Nil.

Op hrs: PPR. HJ.

Met: TOURS (St Symphorien) Tel: 47 29 19 60.

Customs: Nil.

Hangarage: On request to Aero Club. 48 58 03 68   **Maintenance:** Nil.

Remarks: Airfield situated beneath LF-R20C (base 2500'), information on activity from Bourges Twr 119·60 or Paris FIS 126·10.
Avoid overflying habitation in the vicinity.
In calm conditions use Rwy 06.

Fuel: 100LL (1 hour PNR) Sat 1400-SS, Sun & PHs 0930-1200 & 1400-SS	**Tel:** 48 58 04 72 Airfield 48 58 03 68 Aero Club

N4832·73 W00023·02	**BAGNOLES-DE-L'ORNE**	717 ft AMSL
1·6 nm W of Aubigny-sur-Nère.		**CAN 115·40 181 38**

No Radio. FIS — Brest Information 122·80

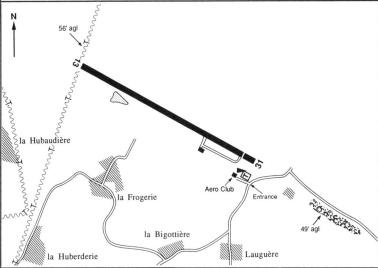

Rwy	Dim(m)	Surface	TORA(m)	LDA(m)	Lighting
13/31	1060x20	Asphalt	13-1060	13-1060	Nil.
			31-1060	31-990	Nil.

Op hrs: PPR. HJ.

Met: RENNES (St. Jacques) 93 31 91 90. **AIS:** DEAUVILLE (St. Gatien) 31 88 31 27

Customs: Nil.

Hangarage: Nil.   **Maintenance:** Nil.

Remarks: Airfield is 3 nm South of LF-R149c (800' agl – 1500' agl) — low level, high speed military training flights.
Circuits LH at 1000'.
Avoid overflying habitation in vicinity of airfield.

Fuel: Nil.	**Tel:** 33 37 91 84 Airfield

N4927·28 E00206·80	**BEAUVAIS (Tillé)**	358 ft AMSL

1·9 nm NNE of Beauvais.

Beauvais APP 119·90. TWR 121·40.   Lctr 'BV' 391·0 (128°/3·5 nm to Thr 13).
VOR 'BVS' 115·90 (307°/1·2nm to Thr 31). ILS Rwy 31 (308°) 'BV' 109·70.

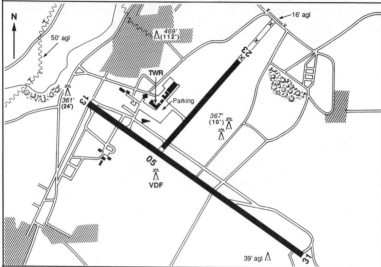

Rwy	Dim(m)	Surface	TORA(m)	LDA(m)	Lighting
13/31	2430x50	Asphalt	13 -2430	13 -2430	Thr Rwy
			31 -2430	31 -2430	Ap Thr Rwy
05/23	1105x40	Asphalt	05 -1105	05 -1105	Nil.
			23 -1105	23 -1105	Nil.

Op hrs: SUMMER 0800-2000. WINTER 0800-2000 (PPR before 1300).

Met: On A/D Tel: 44 45 08 16 or 44 45 18 93 & Lille/Villeneuve.   **AIS:** Lille/Lesquin

Customs: SUM. 0800-2000 & O/R. WIN. SR plus 30-SS minus 30. Tel. 44 45 08 92

Restaurant: Available.   **Hangarage:** Available.   **Maintenance:** Limited.

Remarks: Aerodrome situated within Beauvais CTR (Class E) and beneath Paris
TMA Sector 8 (Class A) — see Arr/Dep Chart opposite.
Special VFR flights are to contact Beauvais App before entering the CTR.
Non radio aircraft and gliders prohibited.
Circuits at 1000 ft., LH. Jet and multi-engined piston aircraft — RH circuits, avoiding
overflying the town.
Night VFR flights permissible.

Fuel: 100LL, Jet A1.	**Tel:** 44 45 12 31 A/D. 44 45 01 06 Operator

BEAUVAIS
VISUAL APP/DEP CHART

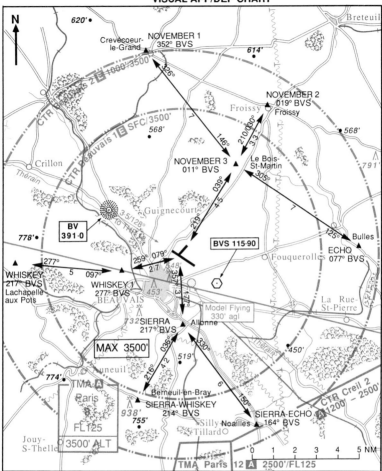

Obtain clearance from Beauvais App prior to entering the CTR. The routes shown above are compulsory for Special VFR flights and recommended for VFR flights.

Special VFR Minima:
Visibility 5000 m (Helicopters 2000 m); ceiling 1000'. (Helicopters 660').

N4719·60 W00311·90	**BELLE-ILE**	164 ft AMSL

2·1nm SSW of Le Palais.   **NTS 115·50 284** 65.   **LOR 115·80 165** 28

MT 398·0 276 47.   **LOR 294·20 165** 28

Lann-Bihoué APP 123·00, 119·70. Belle-Ile Information 118·75 AFIS.
FIS — Brest Information 134·20. Brest Control 118·35

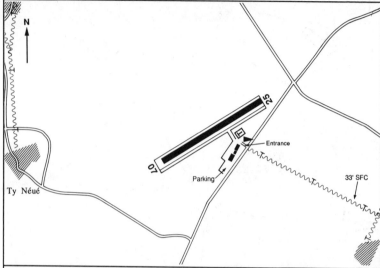

Rwy	Dim(m)	Surface	TORA(m)	LDA(m)	Lighting
07/25	660x20	Asphalt	07 -660	07 -660	Nil.
			25 -660	25 -660	Nil.

Note. Asphalt Rwy is contained within 710x45m Grass Strip.

Op hrs: On request — times variable.

Met: Rennes (St. Jacques) or Lorient (Lann-Bihoué). **AIS:** Rennes (St. Jacques)

Customs: Nil.

Restaurant: Nil.   **Hangarage:** Nil.   **Maintenance:** Nil.

Remarks: App/Dep procedures — see chart opposite. Circuits at 1000 ft. aal., LH on 07, RH on 25. With wind less than 4 kt, use Rwy 25. Airfield surface unusable outside Rwys & Twys.
Airfield may be unusable in poor weather conditions — always check by telephone prior to departure.

Fuel: 100LL.	**Tel:** 97 31 83 09 Aerodrome (not Wed)
	97 31 41 14 Aero Club

BELLE-ILE
VISUAL APP/DEP CHART

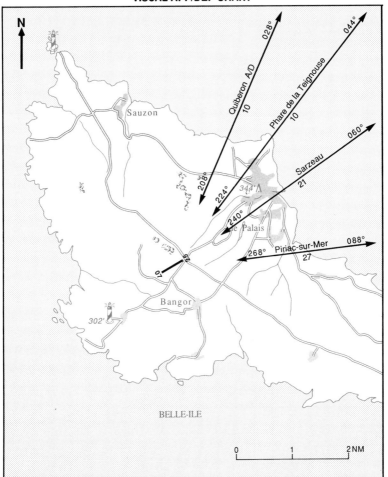

Contact Lann-Bihoué App 123·00 for clearance at least 5 mins before entering LF-D13.
Contact Armor 124·725 for clearance at least 5 mins before entering LF-D18.

Arrivals/Departures from/to the North & North West must route via the following CRPs (as shown on the French OAC 1: 500,000 chart): WHISKEY 2 – WHISKEY 1 – SIERRA 1 – ECHO 1 – ECHO 2; at 700 ft SFC MAX.

N5025·43 E00135·60	**BERCK-SUR-MER**	30 ft AMSL

0·5nm NE of Berck.	LYD 114·05 145 44. DVR 114·95 173 45
	ABB 116·60 333 20. BNE 113·80 228 17

Le Touquet APP 125·30. Berck Club 123·50.
FIS — Paris Information 125·70.

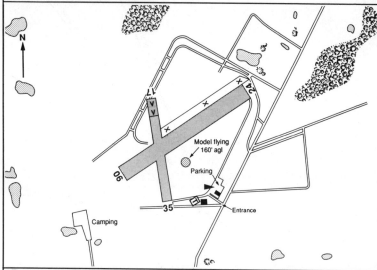

Model flying
160' agl

Parking

Entrance

Camping

Rwy	Dim(m)	Surface	TORA(m)	LDA(m)	Lighting
06/24	900x100	Grass	06 -900	06 -900	Nil.
			24 -900	24 -900	Nil.
† 17/35	600x60	Grass	17 -600	17 -500	Nil.
			35 -600	35 -600	Nil.

† Rwy 17/35 for use only for specifically authorised aircraft.

Op hrs: On request. SR–SS.

Met: Le Touquet or Lille (Villeneuve) **AIS:** Le Touquet (Paris-Plage)

Customs: Nil.

Restaurant: Nil.   **Hangarage:** On request.   **Maintenance:** Nil.

Remarks: Airfield situated just outside the SW boundary of Le Touquet TMA/CTR Class E controlled Airspace. See Le Touquet Arrival/Departure chart for details of Special VFR Route Le Touquet — CRP SIERRA (2 nm E of Berck airfield).
Possible restrictions in use after heavy rainfall, call Le Touquet for info. Airfield unusable outside Rwys & Twys. If no landing 'T' visible use Rwy 24 when wind is less than 4 kt. Circuits at 1000 ft., LH on 17 & 24, RH on 06 & 35.
Gliders circuits at 700 ft., LH on 06 & 35, RH on 17 & 24.
Microlight circuits as for powered aircraft but at 330 ft aal.

Warning: The area is susceptible to sudden seafog, check with Le Touquet and plan suitable diversion to non coastal airfield.

Fuel: 100LL.	**Tel:** 21 09 05 87 Aerodrome
(24 hrs PNR, not available Thurs)	21 31 60 06 Operator

N4906·17 E00034·00	**BERNAY (St. Martin)**	554 ft AMSL
1·6nm NW of Bernay.	CAN 115·40 100 40.	CHW 115·20 339 41
		ROU 116·80 236 36

Deauville APP 120·35. Bernay Club 123·50.
FIS — Paris Information 125·70.

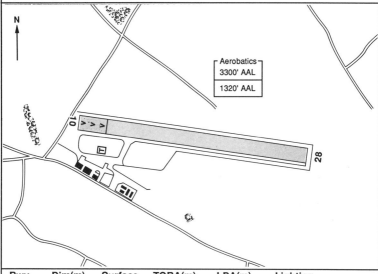

Rwy	Dim(m)	Surface	TORA(m)	LDA(m)	Lighting
10/28	1200x80	Grass	10 -1200	10 -1050	Nil.
			28 -1200	28 -1200	Nil.

Op hrs: On request. SR–SS. Closed Fridays and for the month of January.

Met: Lille (Villeneuve) **AIS:** Deauville (St. Gatien)

Customs: Nil.

Restaurant: Nil. **Hangarage:** Available. **Maintenance:** Limited Tel: 32 43 47 34

Remarks: Airfield situated 2 nm outside the eastern boundary of Deauville TMA
(Class **E**) base 3000' ALT, obtain clearance from Deauville Approach.
Aerobatic Area No.6230 north side of runway 1300' - 3300' aal.
Avoid overflying the town and habitation in vicinity of aerodrome.
Circuits at 1000 ft. aal., LH on 10, RH on 28; microlight circuits at 660 ft. aal.
With wind less than 4 kt, use Rwy 28.
Airfield surface unusable outside Rwys & Twys. May be unusable after heavy rainfall.

Fuel: 100LL (no credit cards).	**Tel:** 32 43 15 62 Aerodrome.

N4740·73 E00112·63	**BLOIS (Le Breuil)**	397 ft AMSL
6·5 nm NW of Blois.	**AMB 113·70 025 16. CDN 116·10 201 24**	
		CHW 115·20 173 49

Blois Information 118·10 (Thu 14-1600, O/T PPR preceding day except Tue & Wed before 1600)
TVOR 'BLB' 109·60 (On A/D).

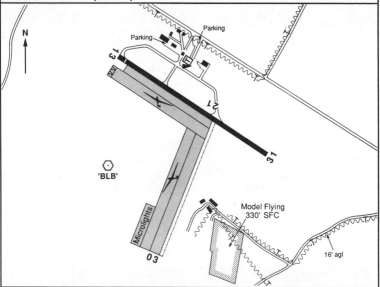

Rwy	Dim(m)	Surface	TORA(m)	LDA(m)	Lighting
13/31	1250x30	Asphalt	13-1250	13-1200	Thr Rwy
			31-1250	31-1250	Thr Rwy
13L/31R	720x60	Grass	720	720	Nil
13R/31L	800x80 †	Grass	800	800	Nil
03R/21L	870x75	Grass	870	870	Nil
03L/21R	870x75 †	Grass	870	870	Nil
† Glider operations only.					

Op hrs: 0900-1700 except Tue & Wed.

Met: Tours Tel: 47 29 19 60   **AIS:** Tours Tel: 47 54 02 81   **Customs:** Nil

Restaurant: Available   **Hangarage:** Nil   **Maintenance:** Limited

Remarks: Circuits at 1000' aal., LH on 13 and 21, RH on 31 and 03; glider circuits opposite direction. Microlight strip on west side of 03L, circuits to the west at 330' aal. Simultaneous use of parallel runways and glider strips prohibited.
Simultaneous take-off and landing of microlights and aircraft prohibited.
Use of grass taxyway on the east side of 03R/21L is mandatory for take-offs Rwy 03R and after landing Rwy 21L; hold before crossing Asphalt Rwy 03/21.
Aerodrome unusable outside Rwys & Twys

Fuel: 100LL	**Tel:** 54 20 17 18 A/D
	54 74 62 22 Operator

N4703.92 E00222.80	**BOURGES**	528 ft AMSL
1·6 nm SW of Bourges		**LCA 112·10 027 24**
		NEV 113·40 260 23

Avord APP 119·70. Bourges Information 119·60 (not available Sun & PHs).
TVOR 'BRG' (058°/4 nm to Thr 06)

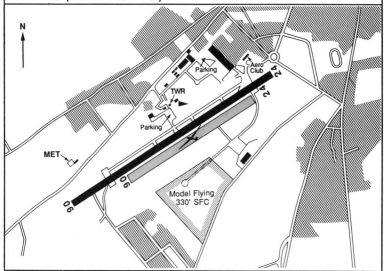

Rwy	Dim(m)	Surface	TORA(m)	LDA(m)	Lighting
06/24	1700x45	Asphalt	06-1700	06-1700	Rwy PAPI 3°
			24-1700	24-1700	Rwy
†06/24	1050x60	Grass	06-1050	06-1050	Nil
			24-1050	24-1050	Nil.
† Rwy unusable 15 Sep–30 Jun due to soft ground.					

Op hrs: Mon-Fri 0800-1830, Sat 0900-1200 & 1400-1730; O/T PPR preceding workday before 1200 hrs.

Met: On aerodrome Tel: 48 50 15 91 — **AIS:** Orleans (Bricy).

Customs: O/R preceding workday before 1800 hrs.

Restaurant: Nil — **Hangarage:** Available — **Maintenance:** Available

Remarks: Aerodrome located within LF-R20A.2 (2100'-FL65), entry clearance must be obtained from Avord App 119·70.
Approach aerodrome below 2100' from NW of a line Bourges – St. Florent (1800' ceiling required). South of this line 1100' ceiling required.
Recommended approach, with AFIS permission, via St. Florent and 'BRG' TVOR.
Circuits LH on 24, RH on 06. Use Rwy 24 during calm wind conditions or when crosswinds prevail.
Simultaneous use of asphalt and grass runways prohibited.

Fuel: 100LL, Jet A1	**Tel:** 48 50 37 11 Twr. 48 67 80 80 Operator. **Fax:** 48 67 80 99.

N4826·87 W00425·20	**BREST (Guipavas)**	325 ft AMSL

5·4nm NE of Brest.

**Guipavas APP 119·50. TWR 120·10. Landi APP 122·40. FIS — Brest Info. 122·80
Lctr 'GU' 338·0 (257°/5·1nm to Thr 26). ILS Rwy 26 (257°) 'BG' 109·90.**

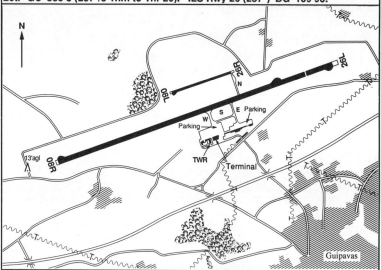

Rwy	Dim(m)	Surface	TORA(m)	LDA(m)	Lighting
08R/26L	3100x45	Asphalt	08R -3100	08R -3100	Thr Rwy PAPI
			26L -3100	26L -2800	Thr Rwy
08L/26R	700x18	Asphalt	08L -700	08L -700	Nil.
			26R -700	26R -700	Nil.

Op hrs: H24. Aerodrome Reporting Office Mon-Sat 0630-1810, closed Sun & PHs.

Met: On A/D Tel: 98 32 55 53. **AIS:** On Aerodrome. **Customs:** H24. 24hrs PNR

Restaurant: Nil.   **Hangarage:** Available.   **Maintenance:** Limited.

Remarks: Brest CTA (Class **D**), CTR (Class **E**).
Routeings depicted opposite are mandatory for Special VFR and recommended for
VFR flights.
Circuits at 1000' aal., LH on 08, RH on 26
With wind less than 4 kt use Rwy 26.
Aerodrome surface unusable outside Rwys & Twys.
Note. Take care not to confuse RWY 26 at BREST with RWY 26 at LANDIVISIAU.
VFR Flights
Prior notice of 1 week required by ATS Brest — Tel: 98 84 60 03 or 98 84 61 11;
Fax: 98 84 86 21; LFRBYDYX or LFRBZPZX. Requests must state:
Callsign, A/c Type, VFR/IFR, A/D of Dep, A/D of Arr (Brest), ETD & ETA.
Delays can be expected.

Fuel: 100LL, Jet A1.	**Tel:** 98 84 61 11 ATC. 98 84 60 03 A/D Office
	98 32 01 00 Operator. 98 84 61 86 Club

BREST
VISUAL APP/DEP CHART

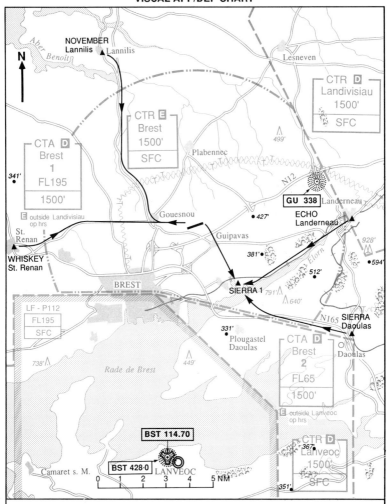

Obtain clearance prior to entering controlled airspace:
- Landivisiau CTR from Landi App;
- Brest CTR/CTA from Guipavas App.

Special VFR Minima:
WITHOUT IFR TRAFFIC — Fixed wing: Vis 1500m . Helis: Vis 800m .
WITH IFR TRAFFIC — Fixed wing: Vis 5000m, cloud ceiling 700 ft SFC.
Helis: Vis 1000m, cloud ceiling 500 ft SFC.

LFPY

1·3 nm E of Brétigny-sur-Orge.

APP 125·57. TWR 124·77. GND 121·92
TACAN 'BY' 110·40 (On A/D) **ILS Rwy 05 (046°) 'BY' 108·90.**

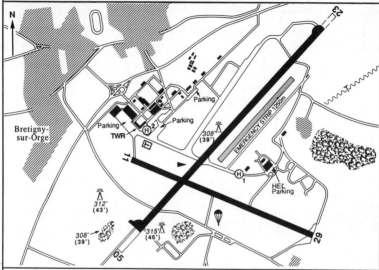

Rwy	Dim(m)	Surface	TORA(m)	LDA(m)	Lighting
05/23	3000x45	Asphalt	05 -3000	05 -3000	Ap Thr Rwy PAPI 3°
			23 -3000	23 -3000	Thr Rwy
11/29	2200x45	Asphalt	11 -2200	11 -2200	Rwy
			29 -2200	29 -2200	Thr Rwy

Op hrs: PPR. *1 VFR* Mon-Fri 0800-1610. *2. IFR* Mon-Fri 0845-1540.
O/T on request preceding day before 1510hrs. A/D closed Sat, Sun & PHs.

Met: On A/D Tel: (1)60 84 05 80. **AIS:** On A/D **Customs:** 24hrs PNR.

Restaurant: Nil. **Hangarage:** Available. **Maintenance:** Available.

Remarks: Arr/Dep and Transit Procedures — see chart opposite and following page.
Contact APP or TWR 3 mins before entering Brétigny CTA, CTR 1 and CTR 2.
Use of airport is strictly by prior permission. Non radio aircraft prohibited.
Circuits RH on 05, LH on 23, 11 & 29.
Aerodrome surface unusable outside Rwys & Twys.

Fuel: 100LL, Jet A1. | **Tel:** (1)69 88 20 42 or (1)69 88 20 40
JP4 (24hrs PNR). JP5 (48hrs PNR). |

BRETIGNY VISUAL APP/DEP CHART

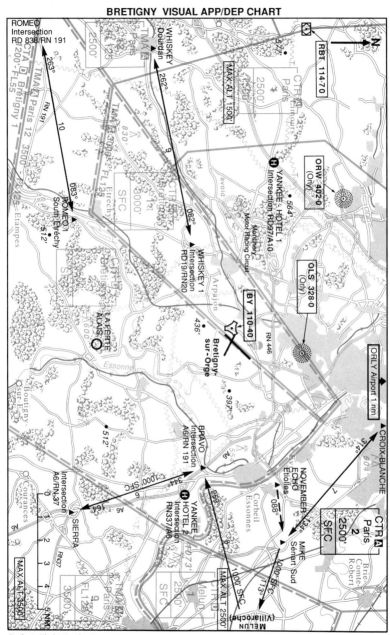

Contact Bretigny APP 125.57 or TWR 124.77 before entering Brétigny CTA, CTR 1 and CTR 2.
Flight Plan mandatory.

Arrivals

• WHISKEY (Dourdan) –WHISKEY 1 at 1000 ft SFC (Helis at 300'). Avoid overflying DOURDAN and BRUERE-LE-CHATEL, circumnavigate to the South.

• SIERRA (A6/RN37) – BRAVO (A6/RN191) at 1000 ft SFC (Helis at 300') . Avoid overflying MENNECY.

Aircraft with speed above 200 kts IAS:

• ROMEO (RD838/N191) – ROMEO 1 at 1000 ft SFC (Helis at 300'). Avoid overflying ETAMPES and ETRECHY.

Departures
Specify required exit point on initial contact with Twr.

• Via WHISKEY (Dourdan). Avoid overflying DOURDAN, circumnavigate to the North.

• Via NOVEMBER ECHO. Avoid overflying BONDOUFLE, EVRY and PONT DE SEINE.

• Via SIERRA (A6/RN37). Avoid overflying LE BOUCHET AREA, SAINT-VRAIN ZOO and MENNECY.

Aircraft with speed above 200 kts IAS:

• ROMEO (RD838/N191). Avoid overflying ETAMPES and ETRECHY.

Special VFR Minima
Fixed Wing: Vis 5 km, ceiling 1500 ft.
Helicopters: Vis 3 km. ceiling 600 ft.

NOTE: All photography prohibited within a radius of 3000 m of Brétigny ARP.

N4736·97 E00246·93	BRIARE (Châtillon)	558 ft AMSL
2 nm SE of Briare.	NEV 113·40 351 28. PTV 116·50 151 39	
	BRG 110·40 033 41	

Briare Information 118·55 AFIS
NDB 'BIC' 405·0 (On A/D).

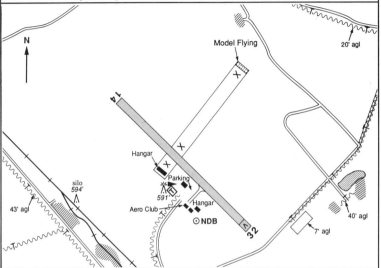

Rwy	Dim(m)	Surface	TORA(m)	LDA(m)	Lighting
14/32	1120x50	Grass	14-1120	14-1120	Nil.
			32-1120	32-1060	Nil.

Op hrs: SR–SS, 2 hrs PNR

Met: ORLEANS (Bricy) or PARIS (Le Bourget).	**AIS:** No provision.

Customs: Nil

Restaurant: Nil	**Hangarage:** Nil	**Maintenance:** Limited

Remarks: Airfield may be unusable during rainy periods, check by phone before departure. Unusable outside runways.
Caution: IFR approaches and departures.

Fuel: 100LL daily except Wednesdays	**Tel:** 38 31 48 07

N4910·43 W00026·92	**CAEN (Carpiquet)**	256 ft AMSL

3·2nm W of Caen.

Deauville APP 120·35. Caen APP/TWR 128·50. VOR 'CAN' 115·40 (On A/D).
Lctr 'CNE' 404·0 (309°/6·1 nm to Thr 31). ILS Rwy 31 (311°) CN 111·10.

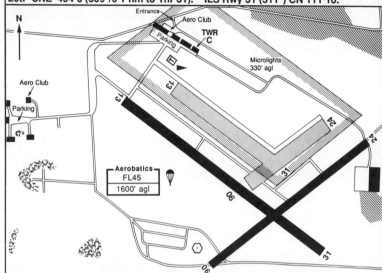

Rwy	Dim(m)	Surface	TORA(m)	LDA(m)	Lighting
06/24	1180x30	Asphalt	06 -1180	06 -1180	Nil.
			24 -1180	24 -1180	Nil.
†06/24	650x100	Grass	650	650	Nil.
13/31	1600x45	Asphalt	13 -1600	13 -1600	Thr Rwy
			31 -1600	31 -1600	Thr Rwy
†13/31	850x100	Grass	850	850	Nil.

† For use of home based aircraft only.

Op hrs: Summer 07-2200 daily, 2200-2400 PPR before 1800.
Winter Mon-Fri 07-2200, Sat,Sun & PHs 08-2000; 22-2400 daily PPR before 1700.

Met: On A/D Tel: 31 26 68 11.   **AIS:** Deauville (St. Gatien) Tel: 31 64 04 04

Customs: Mon-Fri 0900-1800, 2hrs PNR. Sat, Sun & PHs 0900-1200 & 1400-1800,
O/R preceding day before 1700hrs. O/T during Op hrs on request. Tel. 31 26 56 81

Restaurant: Nil.   **Hangarage:** Available.   **Maintenance:** Limited.

Remarks: Arr/Dep procedures — see chart opposite. Circuits at 700 ft. aal.; LH on 24
and 31, RH on 06 and 13. Grass runways reserved for home based aircraft.
Aerodrome surface unusable outside Rwys & Twys.
Caution. Instrument approaches to Rwy 31. Model flying up to 700 ft. agl. 3nm North
of aerodrome. Aerobatic Area No.6300 west side of main runway, 1600 ft. aal up to
FL45. Microlights operating from grass runways, up to 330 ft. aal.

Fuel: 100LL, Jet A1	**Tel:** 31 26 56 81 Aerodrome
	31 26 58 00 Operator

CAEN
VISUAL APP/DEP CHART

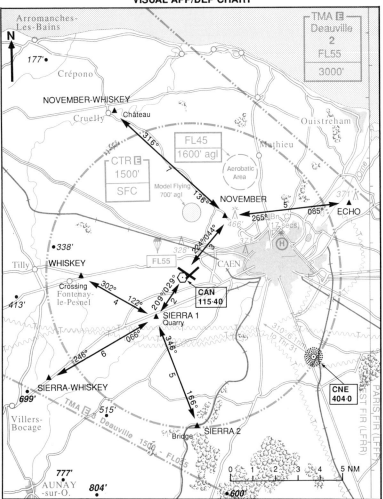

ARR/DEP ROUTES shown above are mandatory for Special VFR flights and
recommended for VFR flights. Routes to be flown at 700 ft. agl.

Special VFR Minima within the CTR
- ARR with IFR traffic: Fixed wing — Vis 2000m, cloud ceiling 700'
                                 Helicopters — Vis 800m.
- ARR without IFR traffic: Fixed wing — Vis 1500m.
                                 Helicopters — Vis 800m.
- DEPARTURES   Fixed wing — Vis 1500 m.
                                 Helicopters — Vis 800 m.

N5057·70 E00157·17	**CALAIS - DUNKIRK**	10 ft AMSL

3·8nm ENE of Calais. DVR 114·95 122 25. KOK 114·50 257 28
BNE 113·80 009 20

Lille APP 122·70. Calais TWR 118·10 *. **FIS** — Paris Information 125·70.
Lctr 'MK' 418·0 (244°/9nm to Thr 24). NDB 'ING' 387·50 (063°/9nm to A/D).

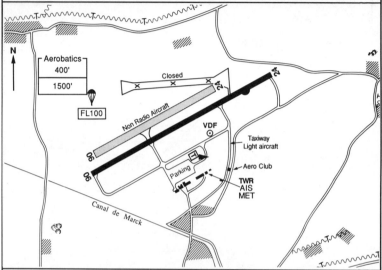

Rwy	Dim(m)	Surface	TORA(m)	LDA(m)	Lighting
06/24	1535x45	Asphalt	06 -1535	06 -1535	Thr Rwy
			24 -1535	24 -1535	Thr Rwy
06/24	1050x60	Grass	06 -1050	06 -1050	Nil.
			24 -1050	24 -1050	Nil.

Op hrs: 0800-1900 daily. O/T (IFR only, except training flights):1900-2100, PPR before 1700hrs. 2100-0800 PPR preceding day before 1700hrs.

Met: Le Touquet and Lille (Villeneuve) **AIS:** On aerodrome

Customs: 0800-1900 daily. O/T PNR — Tel: 21 97 90 66

Restaurant: Available. **Hangarage:** Available **Maintenance:** Nil.

Remarks: Flights within the Calais TMA are subject to the regulations applicable to Class 'E' Controlled Airspace — see page 418. Special VFR flights are to contact Calais App (Lille App if above 2,000') before entering the Calais TMA.
Circuits at 1000 ft. aal; Asphalt Rwy, LH on 24, RH on 06; Grass Rwy, LH on 06, RH on 24. Non radio aircraft must use Grass Rwy. Aerodrome surface unusable outside Rwys & Twys. Demolition Area 1·2nm NNW of A/D, radius 0·5nm, SFC—1650 ft. Parachuting up to FL 100 on north side of A/D.
Warning. Aerodrome susceptible to sudden unexpected sea-fog, diversion to a non coastal aerodrome should be pre-planned.

* TWR frequency outside Op hrs Air/Air in French only.

Fuel: 100LL, Jet A1.	**Tel:** 21 82 71 02 A/D. 21 82 70 59 ATC.
	21 97 90 66 Operator

N4827·53 E00131·43	**CHARTRES (Champol)**	509 ft AMSL

1·3nm ENE of Chartres.   **CHW 115·20 096 21. RBT 114·70 241 22**
EPR 116·65 210 11. CDN 116·10 017 25

Chartres 119·20. FIS — Paris Information 129·62.

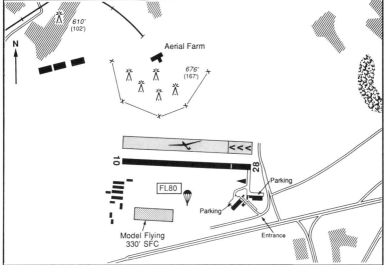

Rwy	Dim(m)	Surface	TORA(m)	LDA(m)	Lighting
10/28	840x25	Asphalt	10 -840	10 -840	Nil.
			28 -840	28 -730	Nil.
10/28	900x100	Grass *	10 -900	10 -900	Nil.
			28 -900	28 -720	Nil.

* Grass Rwy normally reserved for gliders.

Op hrs: On request SR-SS.

Met: On A/D. Tel: 37 21 16 06   **AIS:** Toussus Le Noble (1) 39 56 51 92

Customs: Nil.

Restaurant: Bar facilities.   **Hangarage:** Nil.   **Maintenance:** Limited.

Remarks: Aerodrome situated beneath Paris TMA (Class **E**) FL35–FL55 ; (Class **A**) FL55 –FL125.
Aerobatic Area (No.6430) 3·5nm NW of airfield (1650' agl–FL35), SR–SS Sat, Sun & PHs.
Parachuting up to FL80, 1000-SS Sat, Sun & PHs; DZ on south side of airfield.
Circuits at 1000 ft., LH on 10, RH on 28. Arrange circuit to avoid overflying habitation as far as possible, ie., turn outside the village of Oiséme (1nm NE of Rwy) and inside the road running North from town centre. Avoid overflying the aerial farm just North of the airfield. With conditions of no wind or cross-wind, use Rwy 10. Airfield surface unusable outside Rwys & Twys.

Fuel: 100LL. (0900-1200 & 1400-1900 except Tuesdays).	**Tel:** 37 34 43 48 Aero Club. 37 21 02 20 Operator. 37 34 14 27 Gliders.

N4803·53 E00122·82	**CHATEAUDUN**	433 ft AMSL

2 nm ESE of Châteaudun.

APP 120·80, 119·70.   TWR 118·525, 122·10.   VOR 'CDN' 116·10 (On A/D).
TACAN 'CDN' 116·10 (On A/D).   NDB 'CDN' 359·5 (On A/D)

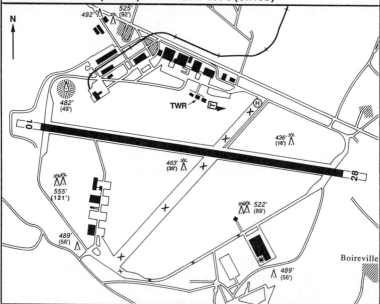

Rwy	Dim(m)	Surface	TORA(m)	LDA(m)	Lighting
10/28	2300x45	Concrete	10-2300	28-2300	Thr Rwy VASIS 2·8°
			28-2300	28-2300	Thr Rwy

Op hrs: Mon-Thur 0830-1700, Fri 0830-1500.

Met: On A/D Tel: 37 45 21 51; and TOURS (St. Symphorien) Tel: 47 29 19 60.

Customs: Nil.

Restaurant: Nil.   **Hangarage:** Nil.   **Maintenance:** Nil.

Remarks: Mil/Civ Aerodrome situated within Restricted Area LF-R89A (SFC – FL55).
Use of aerodrome prohibited outside published Op hrs.
Radio contact with App/Twr mandatory. Arr/Dep as shown on VAD Chart opposite.
Circuits at 800' aal; LH on 28, RH on 10.
Overflying the racecourse (700 m north of 28 threshold) prohibited.
Parachuting to south of runway, Mon-Fri 0600-0800 & 1700-2000, up to FL45.
Aerodrome unusable ouside Rwy and Twys.
Parking of civil aircraft outside published Op hrs on request to Base Operations.

IFR Flight Plans & Messages to: LFOCZPZX and LFJOZPZX.

Fuel: 100LL, Jet A1.	**Tel:** 37 45 09 01 Aerodrome 37 45 65 06 Aero Club

CHATEAUDUN VISUAL APP/DEP CHART

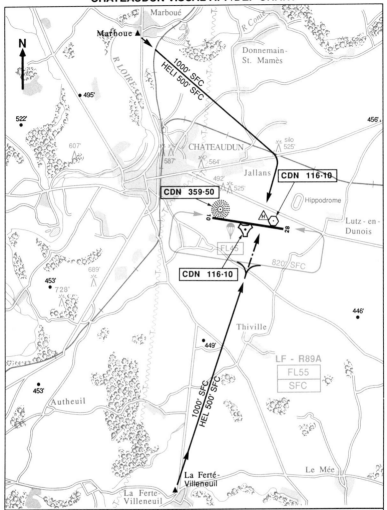

Arrivals — in accordance with the procedures shown above and report to TWR 1 min prior to crossing the centreline of Rwy 10/28.

Departures — as directed by ATC.

Intentionally Blank

N4652·27 E00222·62	**CHATEAUNEUF-SUR-CHER**	551 ft AMSL

2·7 nm ENE of Châteauneuf sur-Cher. **BRG 110·40 159 10. LCA 112·10 044 14**
NEV 113·40 237 28

No Radio. Avord APP 119·70 (Clearance for LF-R20 Zones)
FIS – Paris Information 126·10

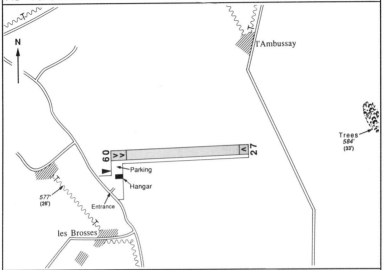

Rwy	Dim(m)	Surface	TORA(m)	LDA(m)	Lighting
09/27	800x60	Grass	09-800	09-760	Nil.
			27-800	27-770	Nil.

Op hrs: On request. HJ.

Met: BOURGES Tel: 48 50 15 91, and TOURS (St. Symphorien) Tel: 47 29 19 60.

Customs: Nil.

Restaurant: Nil **Hangarage:** Nil **Maintenance:** Nil

Remarks: Airfield situated beneath LF-R20B.2 (base 2500'); clearance from Avord App 119·70.
During rainy periods airfield may become unusable due to soft ground; check by phone prior to departure.
During calm or crosswind conditions use Rwy 09.
Airfield unusable outside Rwy & Twy.

Fuel: 100LL Sat, Sun & PHs 1000-1200 & 1430-1800 O/T Tel: 48 60 63 84	**Tel:** 48 60 50 75

LFLX

N4651·70 E00143·35	**CHATEAUROUX (Déols)**	528 ft AMSL

3 nm NNE of Châteauroux.   **AMB 113·70 145 43. BRG 110·40 251 25**
                                                      LCA 112·10 303 20

APP/TWR 125·875, 133·80. AFIS 125·875.
Lctr 'CTX' 428·0 (216°/4·9 nm to Thr 22).   ILS Rwy 22 (216°) CX 110·30.

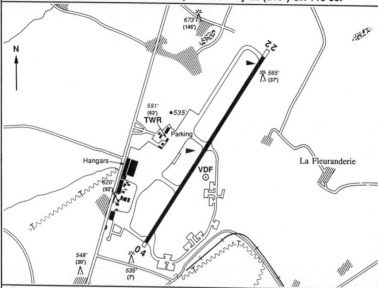

Rwy	Dim(m)	Surface	TORA(m)	LDA(m)	Lighting
04/22	2550x45	Concrete	04-2550	04-2550	Thr Rwy VASIS 3°
			22-2550	22-2550	Ap Thr Rwy

Op hrs: Mon-Fri 0800-1800; Sat Sun & PHs PPR last workday before 1600.

Met: On A/D Tel: 54 22 40 61 or TOURS (St. Symphorien) Tel: 47 29 19 60.

Customs: Tue-Fri PPR preceding day before 1600; Sat, Sun & PHs PPR last workday before 1600 hrs.

Restaurant: Available   **Hangarage:** Available   **Maintenance:** Limited

Remarks: Aerodrome situated within Châteauroux CTR Class E (SFC – 2000'), see Visual App/Dep Chart opposite. Aerodrome prohibited to non radio aircraft.
VFR training flights by military aircraft within the CTR and TMA.
Circuits LH at 1000' aal.
Aerodrome unusable outside Rwys & Twys.
IFR approaches to Rwy 22.

Fuel: 100LL, Jet A1 (cash only)	**Tel:** 54 22 41 38 ATC. 54 22 41 47 Operator

CHATEAUROUX VISUAL APP/DEP CHART

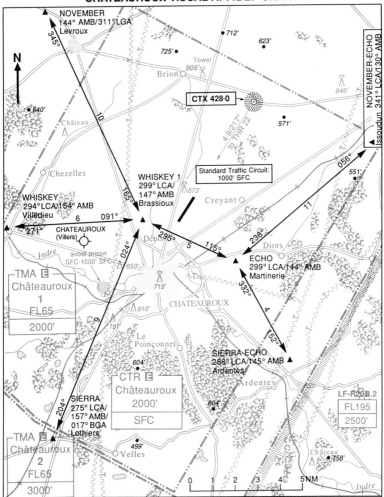

Visual App/Dep Routes shown above are mandatory for Special VFR flights and recommended for VFR flights.

Special VFR Minima:

<u>WITHOUT IFR TRAFFIC</u>

Fixed Wing: Visibility 1500 m.

Helicopters: Visibility 800 m.

<u>WITH IFR TRAFFIC</u>

Fixed Wing: Visibility 3500 m, ceiling 1200 ft.

Helicopters: Visibility 800 m, ceiling 500 ft.

N4650·50 E00137·27	**CHATEAUROUX (Villers)**	541 ft AMSL

3·2 nm NW of Châteauroux.	**LCA 112·10 295 24. BRG 110·40 251 29**
	AMB 113·70 150 42

Châteauroux TWR 125·875 (CTR clearance).

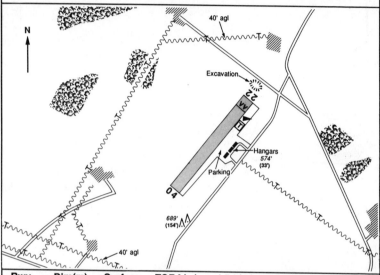

Rwy	Dim(m)	Surface	TORA(m)	LDA(m)	Lighting
04/22	800x80	Grass	04-800	04-800	Nil.
			22-800	22-725	Nil.

Op hrs: HJ Closed Tues.

Met: CHATEAUROUX (Déols)   **AIS:** BOURGES Tel: 48 50 37 11

Customs: Nil

Restaurant: Nil   **Hangarage:** On request   **Maintenance:** Limited

Remarks: Obtain CTR clearance from and maintain contact with Châteauroux App 125·875. VFR minima: 8 km and 1500' ceiling. For SVFR see Châteauroux (Déols).
See Châteauroux Visual Arr/Dep Chart on preceding page.
In calm or crosswind conditions use Rwy 22.
Airfield unusable outside runway.
Caution:
IFR approaches to nearby Châteaurox (Déols).
Cargo aircraft training flights within the circuit area.
Model Flying 2 nm west of airfield, up to 700' SFC.

Fuel: 100LL.   **Tel:** 54 36 68 13 A/D. 54 22 67 45 Club

N4646·32 E00033·12	**CHATELLERAULT (Targé)**	207 ft AMSL

2 nm S of Châtellerault.

AMB	113·70	212	44
POI	113·30	045	15

Châtellerault 120·05. Poitiers APP 124·40
FIS – Bordeaux Information 125·30.

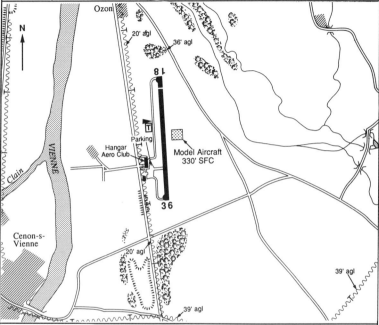

Rwy	Dim(m)	Surface	TORA(m)	LDA(m)	Lighting
18/36	800x20	Asphalt	18-800	18-740	Nil.
			36-800	36-800	Nil.

Op hrs: On request. HJ.

Met: Poitiers Tel: 49 58 22 90   **AIS:** Poitiers Tel: 49 58 24 91/92

Customs: Nil.

Restaurant: Nil.   **Hangarage:** On request.   **Maintenance:** Limited.

Remarks: Aerodrome situated beneath Poitiers TMA (base 1500' SFC).
Circuits at 1000' aal (training at 660'); LH on 18, RH on 36.
Downwind leg to be flown to the East of the village of Targé.
Dep Rwy 18 – After take-off turn left heading 165°(M).
Dep Rwy 36 – After take-off turn right heading 021°(M).
Aerobatics Area (1600' – 3000') 1 nm south of aerodrome, west side of main road running N/S.
Avoid overflying the villages of Targé and Availles-en-Châtellerault.

Fuel: 100LL.	**Tel:** 49 21 00 82

N4939·10 W00128·43	**CHERBOURG (Maupertus)**	456 ft AMSL

5·9nm E of Cherbourg.

Cherbourg APP/TWR 127·30.   FIS—Brest Information 122·80
TACAN 'CBG' 112·50 (On A/D). Lctr 'MP' 373·0 (286°/3·2 nm to A/D)
ILS Rwy 29 (286°) MP 109·90

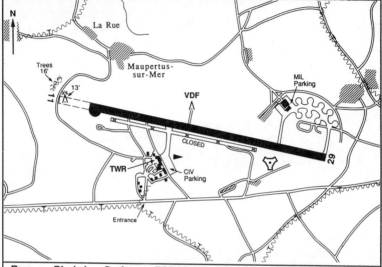

Rwy	Dim(m)	Surface	TORA(m)	LDA(m)	Lighting
11/29	2440x45	Concrete	11 -2440	11 -2440	Thr Rwy PAPI
			29 -2440	29 -2440	Ap Thr Rwy

Op hrs: SUMMER: Mon-Fri 0600-2200, Sat, Sun & P.Hs 0700-2200 (2200-2400 O/R before 1800). WINTER: Mon-Fri 0600-2200, Sat, Sun & PHs 0800-2000 (2200-2400 2400 O/R before 1700).

Met: On A/D Tel: 33 53 53 44   **AIS:** BTIV Brest Tel: 98 40 28 83

Customs: 0800-1900; 1900-2300 O/R before 1800. Tel: 33 22 91 32

Restaurant: Available.   **Hangarage:** Nil.   **Maintenance:** Nil.

Remarks. Arr/Dep procedures — see opposite page.
Circuits standard, at 1000 ft. aal. Instrument approaches to Rwy 29.
Aerodrome surface unusable outside Rwys & Twys.
Warning. Aerodrome susceptible to sudden unexpected sea-fog which may cover the area in a few minutes; check with local Met Office prior to departure. Possible diversion to a non coastal aerodrome should be pre-planned.

Fuel: 100LL, Jet A1.	**Tel:** 33 22 91 32 or 33 23 32 00 Aerodrome. **Fax:** 33 22 90 64

CHERBOURG
VISUAL APP/DEP CHART

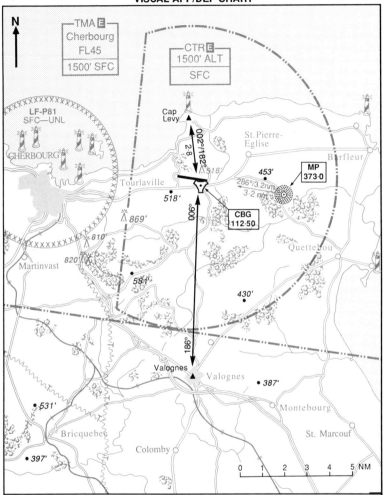

Arr/Dep routes shown above are mandatory for SVFR flights and recommended for VFR flights.

Special VFR Minima:
<u>With IFR traffic</u>: Fixed Wing — Vis 5000 m, cloud ceiling 1000 ft.
Helicopters — Vis 4000 m, cloud ceiling 1000 ft.

N4704·98 W00052·55	**CHOLET (Le Pontreau)**	443 ft AMSL

1 nm N of Cholet	ANG 113·00 186 27
	NTS 115·50 103 30

Cholet Information 120·40. FIS Brest Information 134·20.
TVOR 'CLP' 111·00 (209°/3·4 nm to Thr 21).

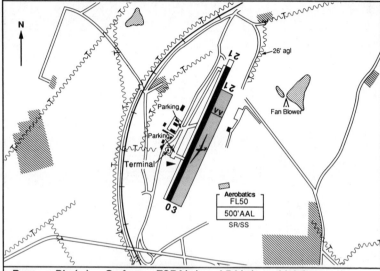

Rwy	Dim(m)	Surface	TORA(m)	LDA(m)	Lighting
03/21	930x30	Asphalt	03-930	03-930	Thr Rwy
			21-930	21-930	Thr Rwy
† 03/21	750x80	Grass	03-750	03-750	Nil
			21-750	21-600	Nil

† For use of home based aircraft and gliders only.

Op hrs: SUMMER: Mon-Fri 0830-1200 & 1500-1900, O/T on request; Sat Sun & PHs PPR preceding work day before 1800 hrs. WINTER: Mon-Fri 0830-1200 & 1500-1800, O/T on request; Sat, Sun & PHs PPR preceding work day before 1800 hrs.

Met: Nantes Tel: 40 84 80 19	**AIS:** Nantes Tel: 40 84 80 45	**Customs:** Nil
Restaurant: Nil	**Hangarage:** Nil	**Maintenance:** Nil

Remarks: Simultaneous use of both runways prohibited.
Entry and exit for grass runway restricted a point opposite the terminal building.
With wind less than 4 kts use Rwy 21.
Possible IFR approahes taking place on Rwy 21.
Aerobatics over airfield 500' aal – FL50.
Model Flying to the East of runway.

Fuel: 100LL.	**Tel:** 41 62 12 22
	Fax: 41 62 29 58

N4926·07 E00248·37	**COMPIEGNE (Margny)**	315 ft AMSL

1·5 nm NW of Compiègne.

MTD 113·65 124 14. CTL 117·60 303 35
CLM 112·90 350 37. BVS 115·90 094 25

Compèigne 123·825 Air/Air. **FIS – Paris Information 126·10.**
NDB 'CO' 553·50 (On A/D)

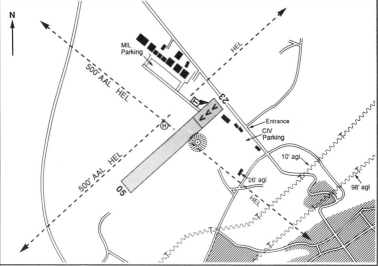

Rwy	Dim(m)	Surface	TORA(m)	LDA(m)	Lighting
05/23	900x80	Grass	05-900	05-900	Nil.
			23-900	23-690	Nil.

Op hrs: HJ. On request.

Met: Beauvais 44 45 08 16. Lille 20 87 51 39.   **AIS:** Lille (Lesquin) 20 87 52 10

Customs: Nil.

Restaurant: Nil.   **Hangarage:** On request.   **Maintenance:** Limited.

Remarks: Airfield situated on the northern boundary of Creil CTR (base 1200') and beneath Paris TMA 12 (base 2500'). MAX ALT 1200' when Creil CTR active ; otherwise 2500'.
Circuits at 650' aal; LH on 05, RH on 23.
Taxy on southern boundary of Rwy 05/23.
Airfield unusable outside Rwys & Twys.
Avoid overflying COMPIEGNE.

Caution: Beware of turbulence from SA330 helicopters.

Fuel: 100LL, as required except Tue & Wed by arrangement.	**Tel:** 44 83 32 12

Intentionally Blank

N4721·68 E00255·15	**COSNE-SUR-LOIRE**	574ft AMSL

2·5 nm S of Cosne-sur-Loire.	**NEV 113·40 001 13** **MOU 116·70 326 48**

AVORD APP 119·70

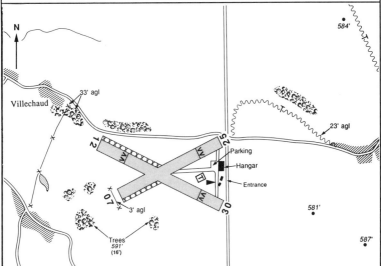

Rwy	Dim(m)	Surface	TORA(m)	LDA(m)	Lighting
07/25	675X60	Grass	07-675	07-675	Nil.
			25-675	25-525	Nil.
12/30	800x60	Grass	12-800	12-610	Nil.
			30-800	30-650	Nil.

Op hrs: On request. HJ.

Met: DIJON (Longvic) Tel: 80 66 51 36.   **AIS:** DIJON (Longvic) Tel: 80 65 49 12.

Customs: Nil.

Restaurant: Nil.   **Hangarage:** Available.   **Maintenance:** Limited.

Remarks: Airfield situated beneath Restricted Area LF-R20 (base 2500' ALT),
contact Avord App for clearance.
Circuits at 1000' aal; variable direction.
With wind less than 4 kt use Rwy 07.
Airfield unusable outside Rwys & Twys.
Caution: Rwy intersection subject to waterlogging in rainy periods.

Fuel: 100LL (HJ except Tue).	**Tel:** 86 28 19 64 (HJ except Tue).

N4921·78 E00009·90	**DEAUVILLE (St. Gatien)**	479 ft AMSL

3·8nm E of Deauville.

Deauville APP 120·35. TWR 118·30.
TVOR 'DVL' 110·20 (301°/6·3nm to Thr 30). ILS Rwy 30 (301°) 'DV' 108·30.

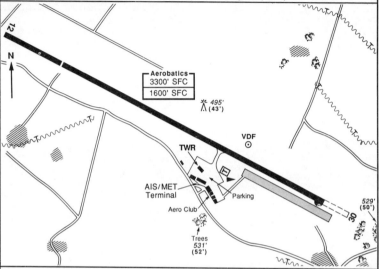

Rwy	Dim(m)	Surface	TORA(m)	LDA(m)	Lighting
12/30	2550x45	Asphalt	12 -2550	12 -2100	Thr Rwy PAPI
			30 -2550	30 -2550	Thr Rwy
12/30	700x60	Grass	12 -700	12 -700	Nil.
			30 -700	30 -700	Nil.

Op hrs: SUMMER daily 0700-2200, 2200-2400 PPR before 1800 hrs. WINTER: Mon-Fri 0700-2200; Sat, Sun & PHs 0800-2000. Daily until 2400, PPR before 1700 hrs.

Met: On A/D Tel: 31 88 28 62.   **AIS:** On Aerodrome.

Customs: 0800-2000; 2000-2400 PPR before 1700 hrs Tel: 31 88 31 28

Restaurant: Available.   **Hangarage:** Nil.   **Maintenance:** Available.

Remarks: Flights within Deauville CTR/TMA are governed by the regulations applicable to Class E Controlled Airspace. Visual Arr/Dep Chart opposite.
Special VFR flights are to contact Deauville App before crossing the TMA boundary.
Circuits at 1000 ft; LH on Asphalt 12 and Grass 30, RH on Asphalt 30 and Grass 12.
Aerodrome surface unusable outside Rwys & Twys.
Note. Avoid the overhead of TVOR 'DVL', except by prior permission from App/Twr at least 5 mins before ETA overhead.
Warning: Aerodrome susceptible to sudden unexpected sea-fog, the area can be covered within a few minutes. Check local MET and pre-plan possible diversion to a non-coastal aerodrome.

Fuel: 100LL, Jet A1	**Tel:** 31 88 31 27 Aerodrome.
	31 88 31 28 Operator

DEAUVILLE
VISUAL APP/DEP CHART

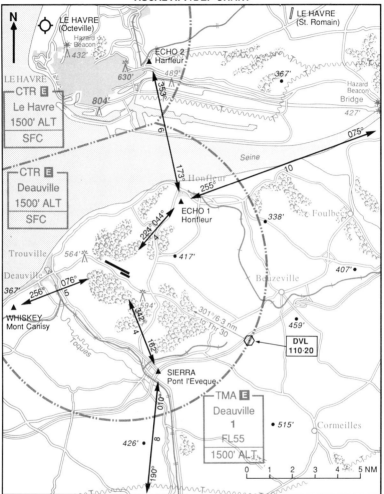

Routeings shown above are mandatory for Special VFR flights and recommended for VFR flights.

Special VFR Minima

ARR (with IFR traffic) — Vis 2000m, cloud ceiling 700 ft.

ARR (without IFR traffic) and DEP — *Fixed wing* Vis 1500m; *Helicopters* Vis 800m.

Routeing ECHO 1 — ECHO 2 permissible only with following minima:

Vis 4000m, Cloud ceiling 850 ft.

See note regarding overflight of TVOR 'DVL' on opposite page.

Intentionally Blank

N4953·10 E00105·02	**DIEPPE (St. Aubin)**	344 ft AMSL
2·1nm S of Dieppe.	**DPE 115·80 238 04. BNE 113·80 219 54**	
	ABB 116·60 246 33. ROU 116·80 348 25	

Dieppe Information 119·00 AFIS (Winter Tue-Sat; Summer Tue-Sun; except PHs).
FIS — Paris Information 125·70.

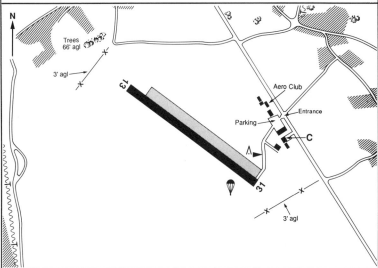

Rwy	Dim(m)	Surface	TORA(m)	LDA(m)	Lighting
13/31	820x30	Asphalt	13 -820	13 -820	Thr Rwy
			31 -820	31 -820	Thr Rwy
†13/31	700x60	Grass	13 -700	13 -700	Nil.
			31 -700	31 -700	Nil.
† Home based aircraft only.					

Op hrs: SUMMER Tues- Sun 0800-1200 & 1300-1800;
WINTER Same hours but Tues-Sat. O/T 24 hrs PNR.

Met: Rouen (Boos) & Lille (Lesquin) & SMIR Tel: 20 47 20 20.   **AIS:** Lille (Lesquin).

Customs: As Op hrs, 2 hrs PNR. O/T 24 hrs PNR. Tel: 33 58 41 40

Restaurant: Nil.   **Hangarage:** On request.   **Maintenance:** Nil.

Remarks: Circuits at 1000' aal., LH on 31, RH on 13. Non radio aircraft and microlights prohibited. With wind less than 4 kt, use Rwy 31.
Parachuting on aerodrome up to 2000' aal., Mon-Fri 1600-SS,Sat, Sun & PHs SR-SS.
Warning. Aerodrome susceptible to sudden unexpected sea-fog, the area may be covered in a few minutes. Check with local MET Office and pre-plan possible diversion to a non-coastal airfield.

Fuel: 100LL.	**Tel:** 35 84 14 40 Aerodrome
	35 06 50 50 Operator

N4835·32 W00204·70	**DINARD (Pleurtuit-St.-Malo)**	217 ft AMSL

2·7nm SSW of Dinard.

Dinard APP 120·15.   TWR 121·10.   VOR/DME 'DIN' 114·30 (On A/D).
Lctr 'DR' 390·0 (355°/5·9nm to Thr 35).   ILS Rwy 35 (355°) 'DR' 109·70.

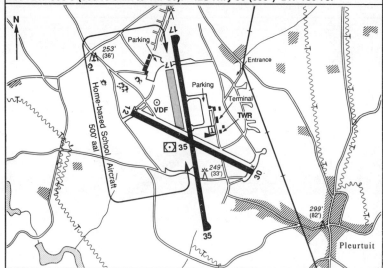

Rwy	Dim(m)	Surface	TORA(m)	LDA(m)	Lighting
12/30	1500x45	Asphalt	12 -1500	12 -1500	Nil.
			30 -1500	30 -1500	Nil.
17/35	2200x45	Asphalt	17 -2200	17 -2200	Thr Rwy
			35 -2200	35 -2200	Ap Thr Rwy
†17/35	670x60	Grass	670	670	Nil.

† Home based school aircraft only, circuits at 500' aal; LH on 35, RH on 17

Op hrs: H24.

Met: On A/D Tel: 99 46 10 46.   **AIS:** On Aerodrome or Rennes (St.Jacques)

Customs: 0730-2030; O/T on request 24hrs on preceding workday.

Restaurant: Available.   **Hangarage:** Nil.   **Maintenance:** Available.

Remarks: Flights within the Dinard CTR/TMA are governed by the regulations
applicable to Class E Controlled Airspace — see page 418 and Arr/Dep Chart
opposite. Special VFR flights are to contact Dinard App before crossing the TMA
boundary. Non radio aircraft strictly PPR.
Circuits at 1000' aal., RH on Asphalt 30, LH on Asphalt 12, 17 & 35.
Instrument approaches to Rwy 35.
Aerodrome surface unusable outside Rwys & Twys.
Aerobatics 1500' aal — FL45 over aerodrome, info on activity from App.
Mandatory prior notification to Twr by telephone for SVFR flights .

Fuel: 100LL, Jet A1	**Tel:** 99 46 16 81 Aerodrome.
	99 56 60 02 Operator

DINARD
VISUAL APP/DEP CHART

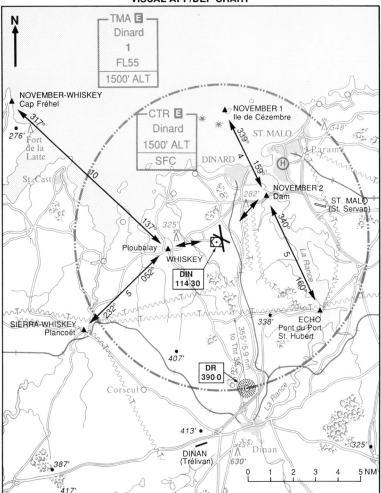

Arr/Dep Routes shown above are mandatory for Special VFR flights and recommended for VFR Flights.

Special VFR Minima

Fixed wing: Vis 5000 m, cloud ceiling 1000 ft.

Helicopters: Vis 800 m, ceiling 500 ft.

Intentionally Blank

N4842·40 E00121·77	DREUX (Vernouillet)	443 ft AMSL
2·1 nm S of Dreux.	EVX 112·40 168 21. RBT 114·70 281 25	
	CHW 115·20 052 20. CDN 116·10 003 39	

Dreux Auto Info. 118·20.

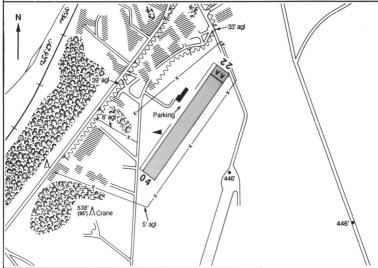

Rwy	Dim(m)	Surface	TORA(m)	LDA(m)	Lighting
04/22	720x80	Grass	04-720	04-720	Nil.
			22-720	22-650	Nil.

Op hrs: On request. HJ.

Met: CHARTRES (Champhol) & PARIS (Le Bourget)

Customs: Nil.

Restaurant: Nil.   **Hangarage:** Nil.   **Maintenance:** Nil.

Remarks: Paris TMA 2·5 nm to the East (base 3500').
Airfield liable to be unusable in marginal weather conditions, always check by phone prior to departure.
Circuits LH on 22, RH on 04.
Training circuits below 500' aal prohibited.
With wind less than 4 kt use Rwy 22.

Fuel: 100LL.   **Tel:** 37 46 26 49

N4822·92 E00204·52	**ETAMPES (Mondésir)**	489 ft AMSL

4 nm SW of Etampes.

RBT 114·70 172 17. **TSU** 108·25 186 22
PTV 116·50 333 15. **MEL** 109·80 265 30

Etampes TWR 119·05. GND 121·85. Bretigny APP 125·575.
NDB 'EM' 295·50 (On A/D). ATIS 129·90.

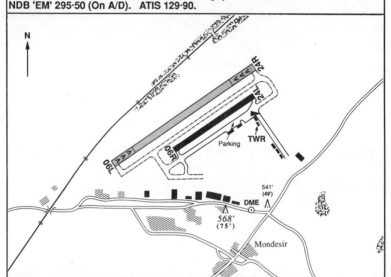

Rwy	Dim(m)	Surface	TORA(m)	LDA(m)	Lighting
06R	700x22	Asphalt	06 -700	06 -700	Nil.
24L			24 -700	24 -700	Nil.
06L	1230x50	Grass	06 -1230	06 -1060	Nil.
24R			24 -1230	24 -1040	Nil.

Op hrs: Mon-Fri 0900-SS plus 30; Sat, Sun & PHs PPR.

Met: Brétigny-sur-Orge or Paris (Le Bourget). **AIS:** Toussus-le-Noble.

Customs: Nil.

Restaurant: Nil. **Hangarage:** On request. **Maintenance:** Nil.

Remarks: Airfield situated beneath Bretigny CTA (Class **D**) Sector 1 base 1200'; see Area Chart opposite.
Aerobatic Area No.6215 on north side of airfield (1600—FL45).
Circuits at 500' aal., LH on 06, RH on 24. With wind less than 4 kt, use Rwy 06.
Airfield surface unusable outside Rwys & Twys.
Helicopter School — training flights home based helicopters.
Avoid overflying LHUMERY (1·5 nm NNE of A/D) and CICHENY(1·5 nm W of A/D).

Fuel: 100LL.	**Tel:** 60 80 95 59 Tower 60 80 95 63 Operator

ETAMPES AREA CHART

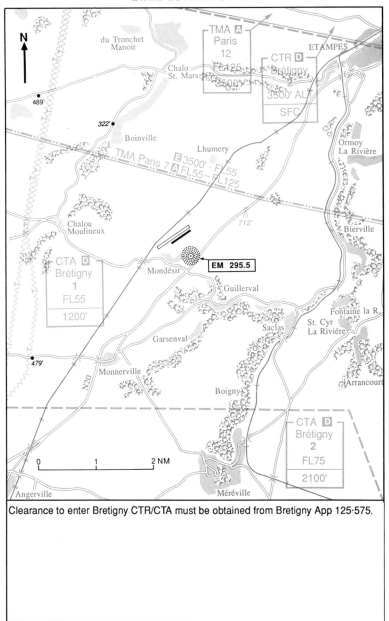

N

du Tronchet
Manoir

489'

322'

Boinville

TMA Paris 7

Chalou
Moulineux

CTA D
Brétigny
1
FL55
1200'

479'

Monnerville

N20

Chalo
St. Mars

Lhumery

TMA A
Paris
12
FL125
3500'

CTR D
Brétigny
3500' ALT
SFC

ETAMPES

Ormoy
La Rivière

E 3500' - FL55
A FL55 - FL125

712'

Mondésir

EM 295.5

Guillerval

Garsenval

Saclas

Boigny

Bierville

Fontaine la R.

St. Cyr
La Rivière

Arrancourt

CTA D
Brétigny
2
FL75
2100'

0   1   2 NM

Angerville

Méréville

Clearance to enter Bretigny CTR/CTA must be obtained from Bretigny App 125·575.

N5004·15 E00125·60	**EU MERS (Le Tréport)**	328 ft AMSL
1·1 nm N of Eu.	**ABB 116·60 261 17. BNE 113·80 212 38**	
	DPE 115·80 053 13	

No Radio. FIS — Paris Information 125·70

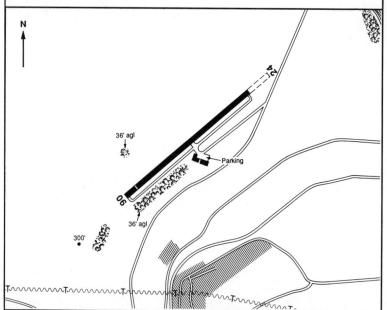

Rwy	Dim(m)	Surface	TORA(m)	LDA(m)	Lighting
06/24	900x30	Asphalt	06-900	06-800	Thr Rwy (PPR)
			24-900	24-900	Thr Rwy (PPR)

Op hrs: Restricted use. Reserved for home based aircraft.

Met: Abbeville Tel: 22 24 05 50   **AIS:** Le Havre Tel: 35 46 38 02

Customs: HJ On request Tel: 35 86 16 49

Restaurant: Available   **Hangarage:** On request   **Maintenance:** Available

Remarks: Aerodrome licensed for restricted use. Reserved for home based aircraft and aircraft based at neighbouring aerodromes.
Caution:
Expect turbulence on short final for Rwy 06.
Terrain depression over first 200 m of Rwy 06, left side runway shoulder does not conform to the prescribed standard.
With wind less than 4 kts use Rwy 06.
Airfield unusable outside Rwys and Twys.

Warning: Airfield susceptible to sudden formation of sea fog. Obtain local Met information in advance and plan eventual diversion to a non coastal aerodrome.

Fuel: 100LL (PNR)	**Tel:** 35 86 16 49

LFOG

N4845·15 W00035·37	**FLERS (St. Paul)**	656 ft AMSL
0·8nm W of Flers.		**CAN** 115·40 197 26
		DIN 114·30 084 60

No Radio.   FIS — Brest Information 122·80

Rwy	Dim(m)	Surface	TORA(m)	LDA(m)	Lighting
06/24	720x25	Asphalt	06 -720	06 -635	Nil.
			24 -720	24 -720	Nil.

Op hrs: On request SR-SS.

Met: Alencon (Valframbert) or Rennes (St Jacques)   **AIS:** Deauville (St. Gatien)

Customs: Nil.

Restaurant: Nil.   **Hangarage:** On request.   **Maintenance:** Nil.

Remarks: Circuits at 1000' aal., LH on 06, RH on 24. Model flying SE corner of airfield up to 500' aal.

Fuel: 100LL.	**Tel:** 33 65 00 53 Aerodrome/Aero Club

N4842·43 E00254·27	**FONTENAY TRESIGNY**	371ft AMSL
1 nm E of Fontenay-Trésigny.	CLM 112·90 210 9·5. MEL 109·80 016 16	
	BRY 114·10 323 24	

Fontenay-Trésigny 120·225 Air/Air.

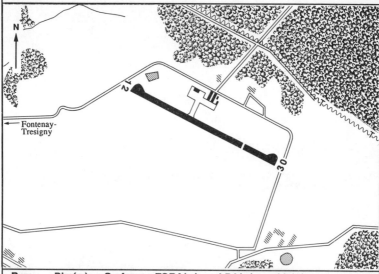

Rwy	Dim(m)	Surface	TORA(m)	LDA(m)	Lighting
12/30	700x18	Asphalt	12-700	12-700	Nil.
			30-700	30-535	Nil.

Op hrs: On request. HJ.

Met: PARIS (Le Bourget) (1)48 62 94 35 **AIS:** Paris NOTAM Office Tel: (1)69 84 56 22

Customs: Nil.

Restaurant: Available   **Hangarage:** Nil.   **Maintenance:** Nil.

Remarks: Airfield situated beneath Paris TMA 12 (base 2500'). Paris CTR boundary 2 nm to the west (base 1500'). Melun CTR 4 nm to the south (base 1500').
Avoid overflying FONTENAY-TRÉSIGNY.
Circuits at 1000' aal; LH on 30, RH on 12.
With wind less than 4 kt use Rwy 12.
Airfield unusable outside Rwy & Twy.

Fuel: 100LL.	**Tel:** (1)64 25 91 45

N4853·03 W00133·68	**GRANVILLE**	33 ft AMSL

2·7nm NNE of Granville.   **JSY** 112·20 143 28.   **DIN** 114·30 056 27
 CAN 115·40 252 47.   **RNE** 112·80 015 49

Granville 118·10.   **FIS — Brest Information 122·80.**
Lctr 'GV' 321·0 (241°/3·8nm to A/D)

Rwy	Dim(m)	Surface	TORA(m)	LDA(m)	Lighting
07/25	960x30	Asphalt	07 -960	07 -960	Rwy
			25 -960	25 -826	Rwy

Op hrs: Daily 0900-1200 & 1400-1800 (Mon-Fri till 2200 O/R before 1600 hrs).

Met: Rennes (St. Jacques)   **AIS:** Cherbourg (Maupertus)

Customs: On request preceding workday before 1800 hrs — Tel: 33 50 12 49.

Restaurant: Available.   **Hangarage** Nil.   **Maintenance:** Nil.

Remarks: Circuits at 1000' aal., LH on 25, RH on 07. Microlights operate from N/S grass strip to the south of asphalt runway, circuits at 500' aal. Night VFR permissible on Asphalt Rwy, night circuits to the North.
Warning. Airfield susceptible to sudden unexpected sea-fog, the area can be covered in a few minutes. Check with local MET office and pre-plan possible diversion to a non-coastal airfield.

Fuel: 100LL.	**Tel:** 33 50 01 44 Aerodrome
	33 50 24 24 Aero Club

LFES

N4803·28 W00339·77	**GUISCRIFF (Scaër)**	564 ft AMSL

0·8nm WNW of Guiscriff.

QPR 117·80 083 21
ARE 112·50 195 17

Lann-Bihoué APP 123·00. Quimper APP 118·30. Guiscriff 129·80.
Lctr 'GIF' 332·0 (On A/D).

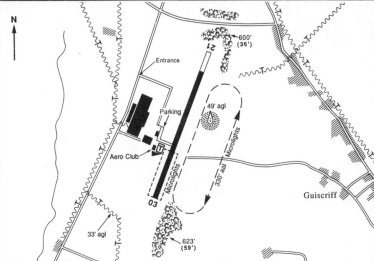

Rwy	Dim(m)	Surface	TORA(m)	LDA(m)	Lighting
03/21	800x30	Concrete	03 -800	03 -800	Nil.
			21 -800	21 -800	Nil.

Op hrs: On request. SR–SS.

Met: Rennes (St. Jacques) or Quimper **AIS:** Quimper (Plugguffan)

Customs: Nil.

Restaurant: Nil. **Hangarage:** On request. **Maintenance:** Nil.

Remarks: Airfield situated beneath Lorient CTA (Class **D**) 3000' – FL115, clearance from Lann-Bihoué App.
Eastern boundary of Quimper TMA (Class **E**) 1500' – FL85 is 2 nm W of A/D, clearance from Quimper App.
Circuits LH at 1000' aal. Microlights operate from southern end of runway, circuits to the east at 330' aal.
Airfield surface unusable outside Rwy & Twys.

Fuel: Nil.	**Tel:** 97 34 00 55 Aerodrome
	97 34 05 23 Aero Club

N4643·12 W00223·47   **ILE D'YEU**   79 ft AMSL

1·9 nm W of Port Jonville   **NTS 115·50 236 41**

Ile D'Yeu Information 118·90. FIS — Brest Information 134·20.
Armor 124·725 (VFR clearance for LF-D18)

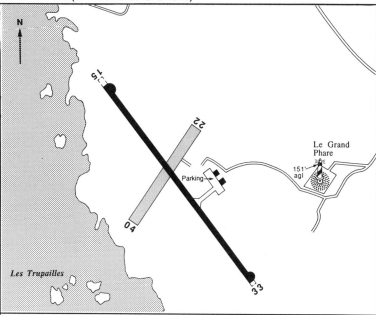

Rwy	Dim(m)	Surface	TORA(m)	LDA(m)	Lighting
15/33	1230x25	Asphalt	15-1230	15-1230	Thr Rwy
			33-1230	33-1230	Thr Rwy
04/22	575x40	Grass	575	575	Nil

Op hrs: 1/4-30/9: 0830-1200 & 1400-1900; 1/10-31/3 PPR (24 hrs) Tel: 51 59 22 22

Met: Nantes Tel: 40 84 80 19. **AIS:** Nantes Tel: 40 84 80 45.   **Customs:** Nil.

Restaurant: Nil.   **Hangarage:** Nil.   **Maintenance:** Nil.

Remarks: Aerodrome is situated within LF-D18, activity state and clearance from
Brest Coperhet callsign 'Armor' 124·725.
Circuits at 1000' aal; RH on 15 & 22, LH on 04 & 33.
Microlight circuits at 500' aal; RH on 04, LH on 22.
Rwy 04/22 for use only when crosswind on 15/33 exceeds 15 kts.
Aerodrome unusable outside Rwys and Twys.

Fuel: Nil.	**Tel:** 51 58 38 22 AFIS
	51 59 22 22 PPR

N4653·32 E00202·29	**ISSOUDUN (Le Fay)**	531 ft AMSL
4 nm SSE of Issoudun.	**LCA 112·10 343 5.**	**AMB 113·70 133 52**
		NEV 113·40 250 40

No Radio.
FIS – Bordeaux Information 125·30.

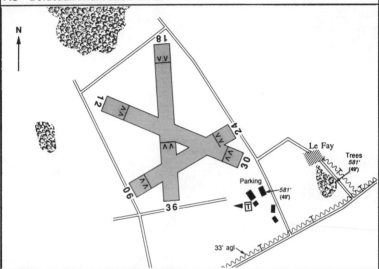

Rwy	Dim(m)	Surface	TORA(m)	LDA(m)	Lighting
06/24	700x100	Grass	06-700	06-600	Nil.
			24-700	24-580	Nil.
12/30	920x100	Grass	12-920	12-760	Nil.
			30-920	30-820	Nil.
18/36	950x100	Grass	18-950	18-840	Nil.
			36-950	36-605	Nil.

Op hrs: On request. HJ.

Met: Tours (St. Symphorien) Tel: 47 29 19 60.

Customs: Nil.

Restaurant: Nil.   **Hangarage:** On request.   **Maintenance:** Limited.

Remarks: Airfield situated beneath Restricted Area LF-R 20B (base 2500' ALT), contact Avord App 119·70 for clearance.
Circuits:
Powered aircraft LH at 700' aal;
Gliders RH at 500' aal.

With wind less than 4 kt use Rwy 30.
Airfield unusable outside Rwys & Twys.

Fuel: Nil.	**Tel:** 54 21 05 38 or 54 21 05 21.

N4845·58 E00039·55	**L'AIGLE (St. Michel)**	787 ft AMSL

1·1nm ESE of L'Aigle.	**LGL 115·00 121 5·5. CHW 115·20 324 21**
	CAN 115·40 121 49. ROU 116·80 214 49

St. Michel Club 123·50.
FIS — Paris Information 129·62.

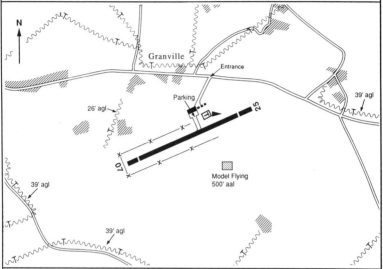

Rwy	Dim(m)	Surface	TORA(m)	LDA(m)	Lighting
07/25	765x20	Asphalt	07 -765	07 -695	Nil.
			25 -765	25 -640	Nil.

Op hrs: On request SR–SS.

Met: Alençon Tel: 33 29 26 96 .   **AIS:** Deauville (St. Gatien) Tel: 31 88 31 27

Customs: Nil.

Restaurant: Nil.   **Hangarage:** On request.   **Maintenance:** Nil.

Remarks: Evreux CTR (Class **D**) 7 nm to NE.
Circuits at 1000' aal., RH on 07, LH on 25.
Home based microlight activity on airfield
Model flying up to 500' aal., to the south of main runway.
Airfield unusable outside Rwys & Twys.

Fuel: 100LL. (daily except Tue & Thu)	**Tel:** 33 24 21 52 A/D (except Tue & Thu)
0900-1200 & 1330-1730, 3 hrs PNR)	33 24 00 59 Operator

Pooley's Flight Guides ©

N4717·37 W00220·78	**LA BAULE-ESCOUBLAC**	105 ft AMSL

1·6 nm E of La Baule-Escoublac.	**NTS 115·50 290 31**

La Baule-Escoublac Information 121·40. Nantes APP 124·90.
FIS — Brest Information 134·20.

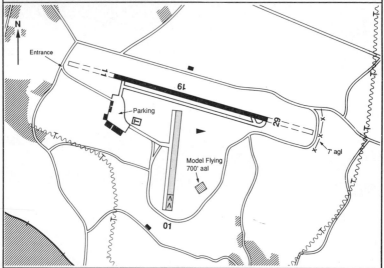

Rwy	Dim(m)	Surface	TORA(m)	LDA(m)	Lighting
11/29	950x25	Asphalt	11 -950	11 -950	Nil.
			29 -950	29 -950	Nil.
01/19	580x40	Grass	01 -580	01 -480	Nil.
			19 -580	19 -580	Nil.

Op hrs: A/D 0900-SS. AFIS & Reporting Office times variable, check by telephone.

Met: Rennes (St. Jacques) or St. Nazaire (Montoir). **AIS:** Nantes-Atlantique

Customs: 0800-2000, O/R preceding workday before 1600 hrs Tel: 40 60 23 83

Restaurant: Nil.   **Hangarage:** On request.   **Maintenance:** Nil.

Remarks: Aerodrome situated 2·5 nm west of Nantes TMA (Class **E**) 1500'–FL195;
obtain clearance from Nantes App 124·90 before entering the TMA.
Avoid overflying Nature Reserve (extending over a large area to the north from 1 nm
north of airfield) below 1000'.
Circuits at 1000' aal., LH on 11 and 19, RH on 01 and 29.
After landing Rwys 11 and 19 clear runway via Twys only.
Airfield surface unusable outside Rwys and Twys.
Model flying up to 700' aal.

Fuel: 100LL (0800-1200 & 1400-1800 daily except Tues 1 Jul-31 Aug 0800-2000)	**Tel:** 40 60 23 83 Aerodrome 40 60 23 84 Aero Club

N4741·65 E00000·20	**LA FLECHE (Thorée-les-Pins)**	115 ft AMSL

2·7 nm E of La Fleche.	**ANG 113·30 079 35**
	AMB 113·70 294 46

No Radio.
FIS – Paris Information 129·62.

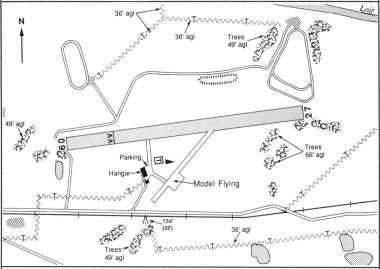

Rwy	Dim(m)	Surface	TORA(m)	LDA(m)	Lighting
09/27	1470x80	Grass	09-1470	09-1170	Nil.
			27-1470	27-1470	Nil.

Op hrs: On request. HJ.

Met: Rennes (St. Jacques) Tel: 99 31 91 90 **AIS:** Nantes-Atlantique Tel: 40 84 80 45

Customs: Nil.

Restaurant: Nil. **Hangarage:** Available. **Maintenance:** Nil.

Remarks: Circuits LH at 1000 ft. Landing direction indicated by Landing T.
Model Flying daily SR–SS, to the south of runway.
With wind less than 4 kt use Rwy 09.
Airfield unusable outside Rwys & Twys.

Fuel: 100LL (Cash only)	**Tel:** 43 94 05 24 A/D. 43 04 05 24 Club.

Intentionally Blank

N4845·30 W00328·40	**LANNION**	292 ft AMSL
1·6 nm NNW of Lannion.		**ARE 112·50 016 26**

Brest Control 125·50. Lannion TWR 118·40, 119·10.
Lctr 'LN' 345·0 (293°/6·5 nm to Thr 29). ILS Rwy 29 (293°) 'LN' 109·50

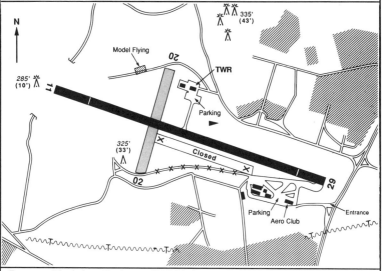

Rwy	Dim(m)	Surface	TORA(m)	LDA(m)	Lighting
11/29	1700x45	Asphalt	11 -1700	11 -1472	Thr Rwy
			29 -1700	29 -1523	Thr Rwy.
02/20	650x60	Grass	02 -650	02 -650	Nil.
			20 -650	20 -650	Nil.

Op hrs: Mon-Fri 0600-2200; Sat, Sun & PHs 0900-1230 & 1400-2000 (1900 Winter)

Met: Rennes (St. Jacques) Tel: 99 65 22 43   **AIS:** Rennes (St. Jacques)

Customs: H24. On request Twr or A/D preceding day before 1600 hrs.

Restaurant: Nil.   **Hangarage:** On request.   **Maintenance:** Nil.

Remarks: Lannion TMA (Class **E**) 1500'–FL55. Obtain TMA clearance from Brest Control 125·50.
Restricted Area LF-R47 (Aerial Farm) SFC–1000', 2 nm NW of aerodrome.
Circuits at 1000' aal., RH on Rwy 11. With wind less than 4 kt use Rwy 29.
Possible instrument approaches on Rwy 29.
Aerodrome surface unusable outside Rwys & Twys.
Unserviceability of Grass Rwy 02/20 will be indicated by white crosses at the threshold of each runway.

Fuel: 100LL, Jet A1.	**Tel:** 96 48 53 04 or 96 05 27 21 Twr.
	96 05 27 21 A/D Manager
	Fax: 96 48 02 56 Twr.

N4610·80 W00111·15	**LA ROCHELLE (Laleu)**	72 ft AMSL

1.3 nm NW of La Rochelle

La Rochelle APP 119·65. TWR 118·00, 118·70.
Lctr 'RL' 322 (278°/3·86 nm to Thr 28. ILS/DME Rwy 28 (276°M) RL 109·55.

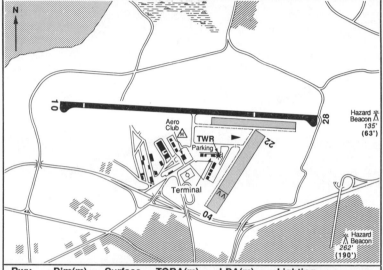

Rwy	Dim(m)	Surface	TORA(m)	LDA(m)	Lighting
10/28	2140x30	Asphalt	10-2140	10-1940	Thr Rwy PAPI 3°
			28-2140	28-1605	Thr Rwy PAPI 3·1°
04/22	730x100	Grass	04-730	04-550	Nil.
			22-730	22-730	
†10/28	690x50	Grass	690	690	Nil.

† Runway reserved for home based aircraft.

Op hrs: Mon-Fri 0600-2300; Sat, Sun & PHs 0800-2200 (Winter 0900-1900); other times PPR before 1500 hrs.

Met: Bordeaux (Mérignac) Tel: 56 34 20 11.   **AIS:** On aerodrome.

Customs: Summer — Mon-Fri (except PHs) 1100-2300 4 hrs PNR Tel: 46 34 85 13, Fax: 46 34 08 92. O/T and Sat, Sun & PHs O/R preceding day before 1900 hrs.

Restaurant: Available   **Hangarage:** Available   **Maintenance:** Available

Remarks: La Rochelle TMA/CTR (Class **E**) — see Visual App/Dep Chart opposite. LF-R49A (3000'–FL65) extends eastwards from the TMA boundary, entry clearance for VFR flights from Cognac App 122·55 (auto responder outside Cognac Op hrs). Circuits at 700' aal; LH on 04 and 10, RH on 22 and 28.
With wind less than 4 kts use Rwy 28.
Microlights prohibited except by special authorisation.
Aerodrome unusable outside Rwys and Twys.

Flying School/Club operated by Blackbushe based "European Flyers" Tel: 46678386.

Fuel: 100LL, Jet A1.	**Tel:** 46 42 05 00 or 46 42 13 30 A/D.
	46 42 30 36 Operator.

LA ROCHELLE
VISUAL APP/DEP CHART

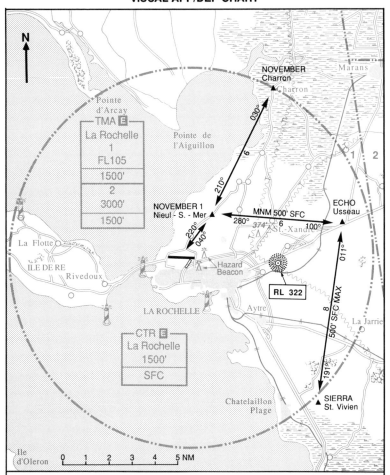

TMA clearance from La Rochelle App 119·65, CTR clearance from Twr 118·00.
Arr/Dep routes shown above are compulsory for SVFR and recommended for VFR flights.
The following altitude restrictions are mandatory:
SIERRA – ECHO Max Alt 500' aal.   ECHO – NOVEMBER ONE Min Alt 500' aal.

SVFR Minima:
Fixed wing — Visibility 1500 m, ceiling 700 ft.
Helicopters — Visibility 800 m, ceiling 500 ft.

Intentionally Blank

N4801·98 W00044·53	**LAVAL (Entrammes)**	328 ft AMSL

2·2nm SSE of Laval.

ANG	113·00	012	30
RNE	112·80	098	40

Laval Information 119·30. FIS — Brest Information 134·20.
Lctr 'LA' 401·0 (326°/4 nm to Thr 33)

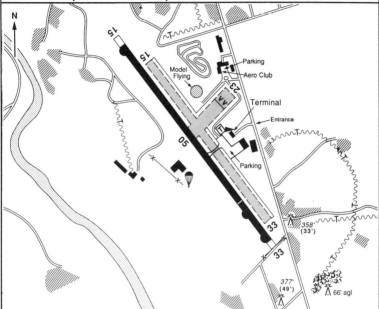

Rwy	Dim(m)	Surface	TORA(m)	LDA(m)	Lighting
15/33	1530x30	Asphalt	15 -1530	15 -1530	Thr Rwy
			33 -1530	33 -1230	Thr Rwy
†15/33	1250x50	Grass	1250	1250	Nil.
05/23	380x80	Grass	05 -380	05 -380	Nil.
			23 -380	23 -280	Nil.

† Usable on prior permission during AFIS hours only.

Op hrs: Mon-Fri 08-1200 & 14-1800. O/T 07-2200 O/R preceding day before1200 hrs

Met: Rennes (St. Jacques) Tel: 99 31 91 90. **AIS:** Nantes-Atlantique Tel: 40 84 80 45

Customs: 0800-2000, on request preceding workday before 1600 hrs.

Restaurant: Nil. **Hangarage:** On request. **Maintenance:** Available

Remarks: Circuits at 820' aal., LH on 33, RH on 15.
Glider operations from Grass Rwy 15/23, circuits LH 15, RH 33.
Simultaneous use of parallel runways prohibited.
Parachuting on airfield up to FL125, SR–SS.
Possible instrument approaches to Rwy 33.

Fuel: 100LL, Jet A1.	**Tel:** 43 53 71 30 Aerodrome. 43 53 02 09 Club.
	Fax: 43 53 93 62 Aerodrome.

N4932·08 E00005·35	**LE HAVRE (Octeville)**	312 ft AMSL

2·7nm NNW of Le Havre.

Le Havre APP/TWR 119·15.   FIS — Paris Information 125·70
Lctr 'LHO' 346·0 (228°/4·6 nm to Thr 23).   ILS Rwy 23 (228°) 'OT' 109·50.

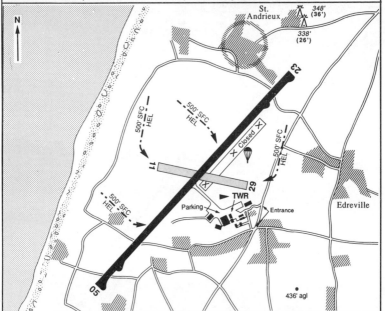

Rwy	Dim(m)	Surface	TORA(m)	LDA(m)	Lighting
05/23	2300x40	Asphalt	05 -2300	05 -2300	Thr Rwy
			23 -2300	23 -2300	Thr Rwy
†11/29	750x60	Grass	11 -750	11 -750	Nil.
			29 -750	29 -750	Nil.

† Unusable outside ATS hours.

Op hrs: Mon-Fri 0600-2200; Sat, Sun & PHs 1000-1900. O/T PPR preceding
workday before 1200 hrs.

Met: Rouen (Boos) Tel: 35 79 00 50   **AIS:** On Aerodrome.

Customs: 6 hrs PNR Tel: 35 46 09 81. Telex: 190382

Restaurant: Nil.   **Hangarage:** On request.   **Maintenance:** Available.

Remarks: Class **E** Controlled Airspace — see Visual App/Dep Chart opposite.
Circuits at 1000' aal., LH on 05 and 11, RH 23 and 29. During calm or crosswind
conditions use Rwy 23. Aerodrome surface unusable outside Rwys & Twys.
Use of Grass Rwy 11/29 on prior permission from ATC.
Warning. Aerodrome may be covered in a few minutes by sudden unexpected sea-
fog. Call well in advance of ETA for MET information. Advisable to pre-plan possible
diversion to a non-coastal airfield. **Note** Heli/Microlight activity as shown above.

Fuel: 100LL, Jet A1.	**Tel:** 35 55 26 00 Operator
	35 48 35 91 Aero Club

LE HAVRE
VISUAL APP/DEP CHART

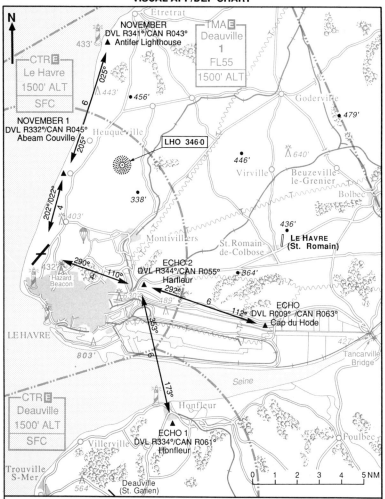

Contact App/Twr 5 mins before CTR boundary, report at N, E or E1 and comply with ATC instructions. Follow the routeings shown above unless otherwise instructed.

Route E1—E2 available <u>only</u> with at least 4 km visibility and 850' cloud ceiling.

Special VFR Minima.

<u>Without IFR activity:</u> Fixed wing: Vis 1500 m. Helicopters: Vis 800m.

<u>With IFR activity:</u>   Fixed wing & Helicopters — Vis 2000 m, cloud ceiling 660'.

Radio Failure:

• Before receiving CTR clearance — do not enter the CTR.

• After receipt of clearance — continue in accordance with clearance to downwind leg.

• Land when cleared by light signals.

LFOY

N4932·68 E00021·67	**LE HAVRE (St. Romain)**	423 ft AMSL
10·8 nm E of Le Havre.	**DPE 115·80 238 39.**	**ROU 116·80 281 36**
	EVX 112·40 316 46.	**DVL 110·20 012 14**

Deauville APP 120·35.   Le Havre APP 119·15
FIS — Paris Information 125·70.

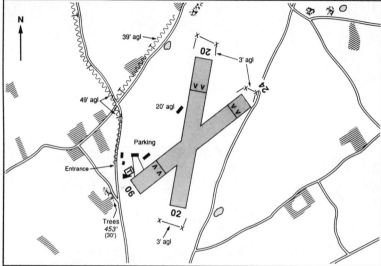

Rwy	Dim(m)	Surface	TORA(m)	LDA(m)	Lighting
02/20	890x100	Grass	02 -890	02 -890	Nil.
			20 -890	20 -690	Nil.
06/24	840x100	Grass	06 -840	06 -640	Nil.
			24 -840	24 -740	Nil.

Op hrs: On request SR–SS.

Met: Rouen (Boos) or Lille (Villeneuve)   **AIS:** Deauville (St. Gatien).

Customs: Nil.

Restaurant: Nil.   **Hangarage:** On request   **Maintenance:** Available.

Remarks: Airfield situated beneath Deauville TMA (Class **E**) 1500'–FL55. Obtain clearance for TMA from Deauville App or Le Havre App.
Circuits at 1000' aal., LH on 02 and 06, RH on 20 and 24. Microlight circuits in same direction at 330' aal. Glider circuits opposite direction to powered aircraft.
Airfield surface unusable outside Rwys & Twys.

Fuel: 100LL (On request SR–SS to Aero Club de L'Estuaire de la Seine).	**Tel:** 35 20 82 61 Aerodrome (not Wed)

LFRM

N4756·97 E00012·18	**LE MANS (Arnage)**	194 ft AMSL
2·7nm S of Le Mans.	**CHW 115·20 228 44. AMB 113·70 316 47**	
	ANG 113·00 065 50	

Le Mans TWR 125·90. FIS — Paris Information 129·62.
Lctr 'LM' 326·0 (024°/3·6 nm to Thr 02). LLZ/DME Rwy 02 'LEM' 109·75.

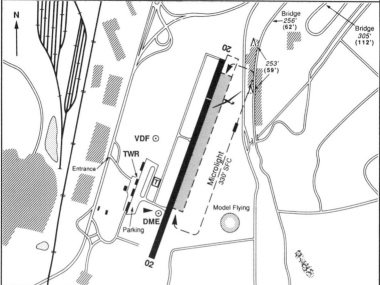

Rwy	Dim(m)	Surface	TORA(m)	LDA(m)	Lighting
02/20	1410x30	Asphalt	02 -1410	02 -1410	Thr Rwy
			20 -1410	20 -1130	Thr Rwy PAPI 4°
†02/20	970x80	Grass	970	970	Nil.
† Glider & microlight runway.					

Op hrs: Mon-Fri 08-2000; Sat, Sun & PHs 09-2000. O/T 24 hrs PNR before 1800 hrs.

Met: On aerodrome Tel: 43 84 00 31.   **AIS:** Nantes-Atlantique Tel: 40 84 80 45.

Customs: Tues-Sat except PHs 0800-2000; O/R preceding day before 1800 hrs.
Sun, Mon & PHs on request preceding workday before 1800 hrs.

Restaurant: Nil.   **Hangarage:** On request.   **Maintenance:** Tel: 43841705

Remarks: Circuits at 1000' aal., RH on 02, LH on 20. Simultaneous use of Asphalt
Rwy and Grass Rwy prohibited.
Avoid overflying LE MANS and ARNAGE.
Aerobatics over aerodrome (1650' agl – 3300' agl) SR–SS.
Glider and microlight activity.
Possible instrument approaches to Rwy 02.
Aerodrome surface unusable outside Rwys & Twys.
Restrictions apply during Le Mans 24 hour Motor Race as notified by NOTAM.

Fuel: 100LL, Jet A1.	**Tel:** 43 84 34 85 Aerodrome
	43 84 10 23 Aero Club

N4859·95 E00156·58	**LES MUREAUX**	89 ft AMSL

1·1nm ENE of Les Mureaux.

PON 111·60 216 07
RBT 114·70 359 21

Pontoise APP 118·80. Les Mureaux TWR 122·95. VDF 120·075.
FIS — Paris Information 125·70 (North) 126·10 (South)
NDB 'LMX' 406·0 (On A/D)

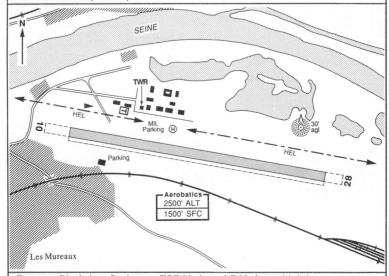

Rwy	Dim(m)	Surface	TORA(m)	LDA(m)	Lighting
10/28	1950x50	Grass	10 -1950	10 -1950	Nil.
			28 -1950	28 -1950	Nil.

Op hrs: Mon-Fri 0800-SS plus 30. Sat, Sun & PHs 0930-1230 & 1400-1830 (WIN) ; 0930-2000 (SUM).

Met: Villacoublay Tel. 46 30 23 88	**AIS:** On A/D	**Customs:** Nil.

Restaurant: Nil.	**Hangarage:** Nil.	**Maintenance:** Mil only.

Remarks: Joint Military/Civil aerodrome situated beneath Pontoise CTR (Class **E**) 1000'— 3500'; see Area Chart opposite. Non radio aircraft, gliders and microlights prohibited.
Overflying the towns of LES MUREAUX and VERNEUIL prohibited.
Aerodrome may be unusable after heavy rainfall – check with ATC prior to arrival.
Circuits at 1000' aal., LH on 28, RH on 10. Circuit pattern — remain South of Rwy axis and the River Seine — see opposite.
Aerobatics over aerodrome 1500' aal to 2500' ALT.
Aerodrome surface unusable outside Rwys & Twys.
Weather Minima: Vis 1500m, cloud ceiling 1000' aal.

Departure Procedures — see opposite.

Fuel: 100LL, Jet A1. Civil aircraft by Aero Club.	**Tel:** 34 74 92 12 Ext 541 Twr 34 74 12 32 & 34 74 21 42 Aero Clubs

LES MUREAUX
AREA CHART

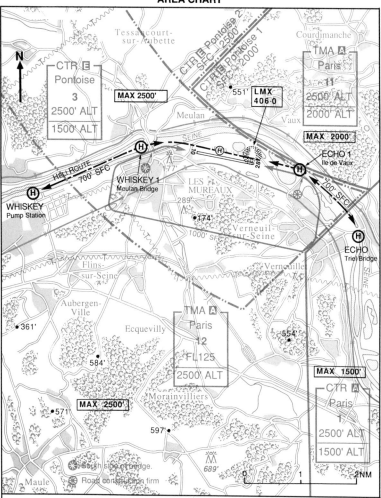

Obtain CTR clearance from Pontoise App 118·80.

Departure Procedures:

Dep Rwy 10 — minimum height 660' agl abeam construction works (between lakes).

Dep Rwy 28 — minimum height 660' agl at southern end of bridge at MEULAN.

VFR Minima: Vis 1500 m, cloud ceiling 1000 ft

Intentionally Blank

N4912·18 W00130·40	**LESSAY**	92 ft AMSL
1·3nm SE of Lessay.	**JSY 112·20 098 21. CAN 115·40 277 41**	
	DIN 114·30 037 43	

No Radio. FIS — Brest Information 122·80.

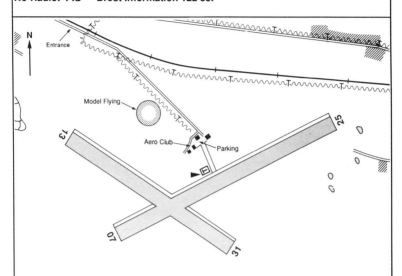

Rwy	Dim(m)	Surface	TORA(m)	LDA(m)	Lighting
07/25	1268x80	Grass	07 -1268	07 -1268	Nil.
			25 -1268	25 -1268	Nil.
13/31	1004x80	Grass	13 -1004	13 -1004	Nil.
			31 -1004	31 -1004	Nil.

Op hrs: On request SR–SS.

Met: Cherbourg (Maupertus) or Rennes (St. Jacques) **AIS:** NOTAMs (Aero Club).

Customs: Nil.

Restaurant: Nil. **Hangarage:** On request. **Maintenance:** Nil.

Remarks: Circuits LH at 1000' aal. With wind less than 4 kts use Rwy 25. Gliders operating LH circuits at 1000', inside powered aircraft circuits.
Model flying up to 500' aal.
Use of airfield may be restricted after heavy rainfall.
Warning. Possibility of sudden unexpected sea-fog, airfield can become covered within a few minutes. Obtain latest local MET information prior to departure and pre-plan possible diversion to a non coastal airfield.

Fuel: 100LL. (Sat pm, Sun & PHs).	**Tel:** 33 46 44 22 (Sat pm, Sun & PHs)

| N5030·90 E00137·68 | **LE TOUQUET** | 36 ft AMSL |

| 1·5nm ESE of Le Touquet. | DVR 114·95 169 40. LYD 114·05 140 41 |
| | BNE 113·80 242 12·5 |

APP 125·30, 118·30. TWR 118·30, 125·30
Lctr 'LT' 358·0 (138°/1·08nm to Thr 14). ILS Rwy 14 (138°) 'LT' 109·10.

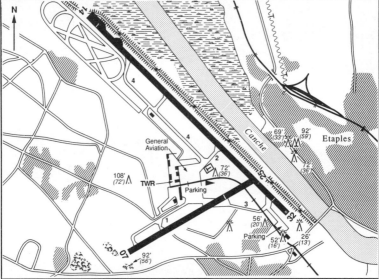

Rwy	Dim(m)	Surface	TORA(m)	LDA(m)	Lighting
07/25	1200x40	Asphalt	07 -1200	07 -1200	Nil.
			25 -1200	25 -900	Nil.
14/32	2250x40	Asphalt	14 -2250	14 -2150	Ap Thr Rwy
			32 -2250	32 -2100	Thr Rwy AVASIS 3°

Op hrs: WINTER 0800-2000; SUMMER 0800-2000. O/T commercial flights only, on request to LFATYDYX before 1600 (Winter), 1700 (Summer).

Met: On A/D Tel: 21 05 13 55. **AIS:** On Aerodrome. **Customs:** As Op hrs.

Restaurant: Available. **Hangarage:** Available. **Maintenance:** Available.

Remarks: Flights within Le Touquet TMA/CTR are governed by the rules applicable to Class 'E' controlled airspace. Special VFR flights are to contact Le Touquest App for clearance before entering the TMA. The SVFR routes depicted opposite are mandatory for SVFR flights and recommeded for all VFR flighjts.
Circuits at 1000' aal, LH on 14 and 25, RH on 07 and 32.
Non radio aircraft PPR by telephone. SVFR not available to non radio aircraft.
Departures Call Le Touquet Ground 118·30 before starting engines.
Warning. Possibility of sudden unexpected sea-fog. Call aerodrome prior to departure for local MET information. Advisable to pre-plan possible diversion to a non coastal aerodrome.

| **Fuel:** 100/130, Jet A1. | **Tel:** 21 05 00 66 ATC. |
| (Total credit card or cash). | 21 05 03 99 Operator |

LE TOUQUET
VISUAL APP/DEP CHART

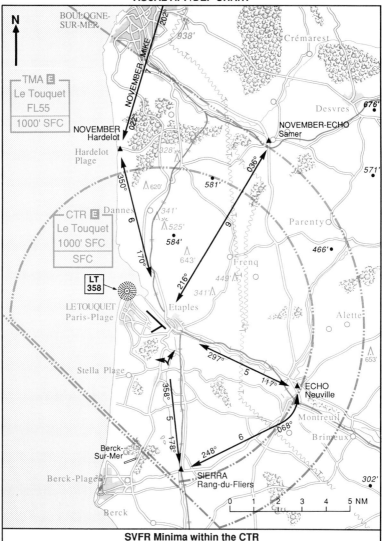

N

BOULOGNE-SUR-MER

TMA **E**
Le Touquet
FL55
1000' SFC

NOVEMBER-MIKE
202°
022°

938'

Crémarest

Desvres

676'

NOVEMBER
Hardelot

Hardelot Plage

NOVEMBER-ECHO
Samer

036°

571'

328'

350°
6

CTR **E**
Le Touquet
1000' SFC
SFC

Dannes

341'

620'

525'

581'

Parenty

466'

170°

584'

643'

Frenq

LT
358

216°

449'

341'

Alette

LE TOUQUET
Paris-Plage

Etaples

653'

Stella Plage

297°
5

117°

ECHO
Neuville

358°
5

068°

Montreuil
Brimeux

178°

248°
6

Berck-Sur-Mer

SIERRA
Rang-du-Fliers

302'

Berck-Plage

0 1 2 3 4 5 NM

Berck

SVFR Minima within the CTR

Fixed Wing
- ARR — Vis 3 km ceiling 820'
- DEP — Vis 1500 m ceiling 660'

Helicopters
- ARR/DEP — Vis 800 m ceiling 660'

N5033·85 E00305·32	**LILLE (Lesquin)**	157 ft AMSL

3 nm SSE of Lille.

APP 127·90, 122·70. TWR 118·55, 122·70. GND 121·80. TVOR 'LEQ' 109·60
Lctr 'LL' 332·0 (259°/3·84 nm to Thr 26). ILS Rwy 26 (259°) LL 110·10

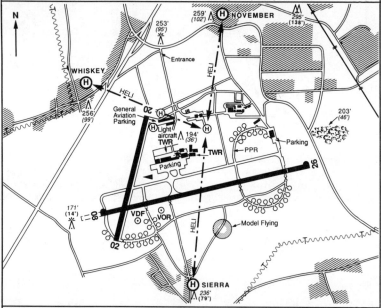

Rwy	Dim(m)	Surface	TORA(m)	LDA(m)	Lighting
02/20	1600x30	Asphalt	02 -1600	02 -1600	Thr Rwy
			20 -1600	20 -1600	Thr Rwy
08/26	2825x45	Asphalt	08 -2825	08 -2825	Thr Rwy PAPI 3·9°
			26 -2825	26 -2545	Ap Thr Rwy
					IBn "L"

Op hrs: H24. Reporting Office and AIS closed Sun & Mon nights and nights preceding Public Holidays.

Met: On aerodrome, Tel: 20 87 51 39.   **AIS:** On Aerodrome.

Customs: 0600-2300, other times O/R before 1800 hrs.

Restaurant: Available.   **Hangarage:** Available.   **Maintenance:** Available.

Remarks: Lille TMA/CTR (Class **D**) Controlled Airspace.
ARR/DEP procedures — see page opposite.
Prior notification mandatory for SVFR flights.
Non radio aircraft and gliders prohibited.
Circuits at 1000' aal.
Aerodrome surface unusable outside Rwys & Twys.

Fuel: 100LL, Jet A1.	**Tel:** 20 87 52 10 Aerodrome & AIS
	20 51 52 88 Operator

LILLE
VISUAL APP/DEP CHART

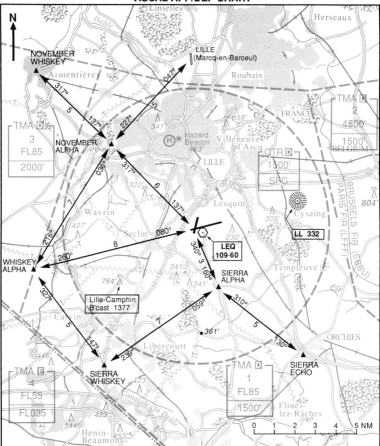

Obtain clearance for controlled airspace before entering Lille TMA.

Arrival/Departure Routes depicted above are mandatory for Special VFR Flights and recommended for all VFR flights.

Special VFR Minima

Fixed wing: Vis 5 km, ceiling 1000 ft.

Helicopters: Vis 800 m, ceiling 500 ft.

Note: Transponder mandatory for SVFR flights.

Intentionally Blank

N5041·28 E00304·60	**LILLE (Marcq-en-Barœul)**	69 ft AMSL

2·7nm N of Lille.	**KOK** 114·50 149 29.	**CMB** 112·60 356 28
	AFI 114·90 256 43.	**BNE** 113·80 088 45

Lille APP 127·90, 122·70. Lille Marcq 122·00
FIS — Paris Information 125·70.

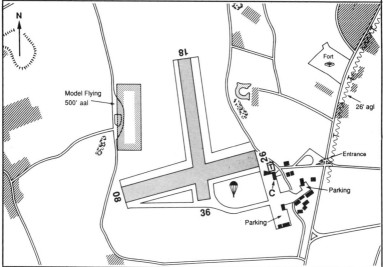

Rwy	Dim(m)	Surface	TORA(m)	LDA(m)	Lighting
08/26	850x100	Grass	08 -850	08 -850	Nil.
			26 -850	26 -850	Nil.
18/36	850x80	Grass	18 -850	18 -850	Nil.
			36 -850	36 -850	Nil.

Op hrs: Mon, Tue & Fri (except PHs) 0900-1200 & 1400-1700;
Sat, Sun & PHs 0900-1200 & 1400-SS.

Met: Lille (Lesquin) Tel: 20 87 51 39   **AIS:** Lille (Lesquin) Tel: 20 87 52 10

Customs: Nil.

Restaurant: Nil.   **Hangarage:** On request.   **Maintenance:** Limited.

Remarks: Airfield situated 1 nm outside northern boundary of Lille TMA/CTR (Class **D**).
Circuits at 1000' aal., LH on 18, 36 & 26, RH on 08; gliders and microlights opposite
direction; gliders at 700', microlights at 500'.
Non radio aircraft prohibited Sat, Sun & PHs. With wind less than 4 kts, use Rwy 36.
Model flying up to 500' aal on west side of airfield.
Aerobatics Area 1 nm W of airfield 1600'–FL45.
Airfield surface unusable outside Rwys & Twys.

Use of Twys
• Twy North of Rwy 08/26 reserved for gliders when Rwy 08/26 is in use.
• Twy West of Rwy 18/36 reserved for gliders when Rwy 18 is in use.
• Twy East of Rwy 18/36 reserved for gliders when Rwy 18 is in use.

Fuel: 100LL.	**Tel:** 20 72 18 07 A/D (except Wed & Thu)
	20 72 40 98 Aero Club

LFPL

N4849·38 E00237·43	**LOGNES (Emerainville)**	354 ft AMSL

0·8 nm S of Lognes.

CLM 112·90 269 15.	**BRY** 114·10 316 37
OL 111·20 062 11.	**CTL** 117·60 246 42

Lognes TWR 118·60. GND 121·85. ATIS 129·425.
FIS —Paris Information 126·10.

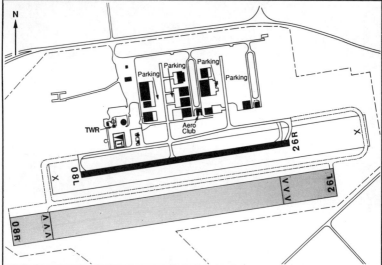

Rwy	Dim(m)	Surface	TORA(m)	LDA(m)	Lighting
08L/26R	700x20	Asphalt	08 -700	08 -700	Nil.
			26 -700	26 -700	PAPI 3·59°
08R/26L	1100x100	Grass	08 -1100	08 -960	Nil.
			26 -1100	26 -920	Nil.

Op hrs: 0900-SS plus 30 daily.

Met: Paris (Le Bourget) Tel: (1) 48 35 99 98 **AIS:** Paris (Le Bourget) (1) 48 62 53 14

Customs: Tue - Fri 24 hrs PNR; Sat, Sun & Mon on request Fri before 1400 hrs.

Restaurant: Available. **Hangarage:** On request.

Maintenance: Available.

Remarks: Airfield situated beneath Paris CTR (Class **A**) 1500'–2500' — see Area
Chart on opposite page.
Non radio aircraft strictly PPR.
Circuits at 850' aal., LH on 08L&R, RH 26L&R. Adhere to circuit pattern shown
opposite. With wind less than 4 kts, use Rwy 26R.
Possible turbulence on final approach to Rwys 26L&R with winds W or SW.
Shoulders of Asphalt Rwy 08L/26R prohibited for taxying.
Airfield surface unusable outside Rwys & Twys.
Avoid overflying Château de la Malnoue (0·7 nm WNW of airfield).
Helicopters Arr/Dep at 700' aal.
Training flights and local helicopter flights prohibited.

Fuel: 100LL, Jet A1.	**Tel:** 60 05 37 57 or 60 05 38 55

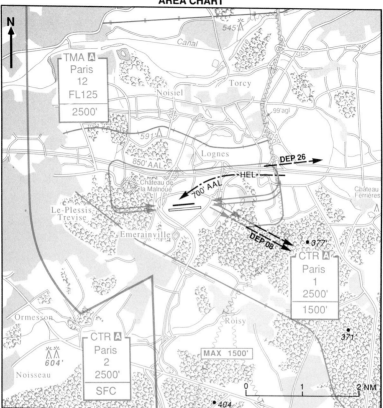

Arr/Dep Procedures:

Routeing from/to the North East through East to South — as instructed by ATC, MAX ALT 1500'.

From/to the Northwest via the VFR Transit Route ECHO 1 – ECHO 2 – WHISKEY 2 – WHISKEY 1 (See PARIS/Le Bourget).

SVFR Minima: Vis 5 km, ceiling 1500 ft.

N4702·23 E00006·08	**LOUDUN**	315 ft AMSL

1·5 nm NNE of Loudun.	**AMB 113·70 243 46**
	POI 113·30 347 29

No Radio.
FIS – Bordeaux Information 122·80

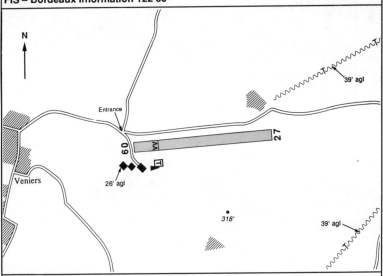

Rwy	Dim(m)	Surface	TORA(m)	LDA(m)	Lighting
09/27	790x60	Grass	09-790	09-630	Nil.
			27-790	27-790	Nil.

Op hrs: On request. HJ.

Met: Poitiers 49 58 24 91 & Bordeaux 56 34 20 11. **AIS:** Poitiers (Biard) 4958 24 91

Customs: Nil

Restaurant: Nil.   **Hangarage:** Nil.   **Maintenance:** Nil.

Remarks: Restricted Area LF-R149B (800' – 1500' agl) 4 nm to the South.
Circuits LH at 1000' aal.
With wind less than 4 kt use Rwy 27.
Airfield unusable outside Rwy.

Fuel: 100LL. HJ except Tue.	**Tel:** 49 98 12 81

N5037·28 E00238·77	**MERVILLE (Calonne)**	59 ft AMSL
1·6 nm S of Merville	KOK 114·50 183 28. CMB 112.60 322 32	
	BNE 113·80 094 29	

Lille APP 127·90. Merville TWR 119·075. NDB 'MRV' 404·0 (220°/3·8 nm to Thr 22). NDB 'MVC' 327·0 (039°/3·07 nm to Thr 04)

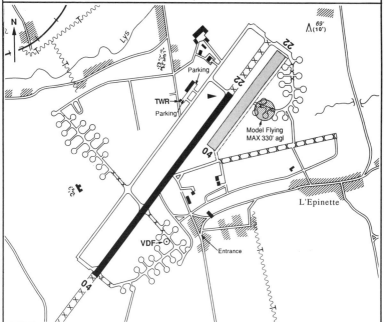

Rwy	Dim(m)	Surface	TORA(m)	LDA(m)	Lighting
04/22	1850x45	Asphalt/	04 -1850	04 -1850	Thr Rwy
		Concrete	22 -1850	22 -1850	Thr Rwy PAPI
04/22	1000x80	Grass	04 -1000	04 -1000	Nil
			22 -1000	22 -1000	Nil

Op hrs: Mon-Fri 0800-2000. Other times O/R before 1500 hrs previous working day.

Met: Lille (Villeneuve) Tel: 20 47 20 20   **AIS:** Lille (Lesquin) Tel: 20 87 52 10

Customs: Mon-Fri 12-2000 (4 hrs prior notice).
Sat, Sun & PHs (prior notice previous working day before 1500 hrs).

Restaurant: Nil	**Hangarage:** Nil	**Maintenance:** Available

Remarks: A/D situated beneath Lille TMA (Class **E**) base 1500'; TMA clearance from Lille App. Circuits at 1000'; LH on 22, RH on 04. Circuits for Grass Rwy inside standard circuit. Traffic using Grass Rwy are not controlled by ATC but entry and exit to traffic pattern must be notified to ATC. With wind less than 4 kt use Rwy 04.
Caution. Narrow taxiways to parking areas. Possible instrument approaches to Rwy 04. No access to Grass Rwy via taxiways to the East of Grass Rwy.
Surface unusable outside Rwys & Twys.

Fuel: 100LL (Cash)	**Tel:** 28 48 30 50 A/D, 28 49 64 27 Twr.
	21 26 17 09 Club.

N46 55·98 W00119·53	**MONTAIGU (St. Georges)**	184ft AMSL

2·7 nm S of Montaigu.	**NTS 115·50 141 18**
	ANG 113·00 211 41

No Radio. Nantes APP 124·90.
FIS – Brest Information 134·20.

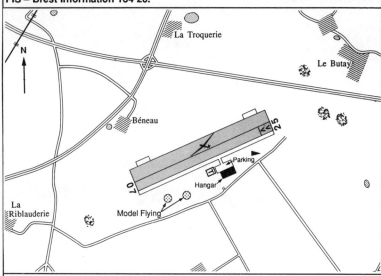

La Troquerie

Le Butay

Béneau

07/25

Parking

Hangar

La Riblauderie

Model Flying

Rwy	Dim(m)	Surface	TORA(m)	LDA(m)	Lighting
07/25	900x60	Grass	07-900	09-900	Nil.
			25-900	25-825	Nil.

Op hrs: On request. HJ.

Met: Nantes (Atlantique) 40 84 80 19   **AIS:** Nantes (Atlantique) 40 84 80 45.

Customs: Nil.

Restaurant: Nil.   **Hangarage:** Nil.   **Maintenance:** Nil.

Remarks: Airfield situated beneath Nantes TMA 3 (base 3000' ALT), and 1 nm SE of TMA 2 (base 1500').
Glider strip to north and parallel to Rwy 07/25. Simultaneous use of runway and glider strip prohibited.
Powered aircraft circuits to the South at 1000' aal., glider circuits to the North at 1000' aal.
Airfield unusable outside Rwy, Twy and Parking Area.

Fuel: Nil.	**Tel:** 51 42 08 94

N47 57·63 E00241·15	**MONTARGIS (Vimory)**	308 ft AMSL

2·7 nm SW of Montargis.

PTV 116·50 128 21. MEL 109·80 193 30
BRY 114·10 225 36

Montargis 123·50 Air/Air
FIS – Paris Information 126·10

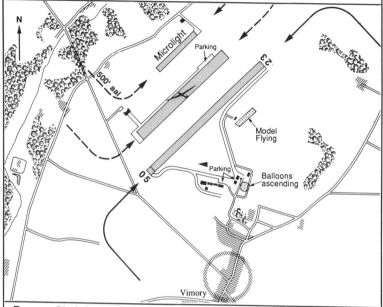

Rwy	Dim(m)	Surface	TORA(m)	LDA(m)	Lighting
05/23	1200x50	Grass	05-1200	05-1160	Nil.
			23-1200	23-1200	Nil.

Op hrs: On request. HJ.

Met: PARIS (Le Bourget) (1) 48 35 99 98.　　**AIS:** Bourges.

Customs: Nil.

Restaurant: Nil　　**Hangarage:** On request　**Maintenance:** Nil.

Remarks: Circuits at 1000' aal; RH on 05, LH on 23.
Glider strip (900 x 80 m) to the NW of, and parallel to Rwy 05/23.
　Glider circuits LH on 05, RH on 23.
Microlight Strip (400 x 40 m) to the NW of, and parallel to the Glider Strip.
　Microlight circuits inside glider circuits at 500' aal.
Model Flying Area (SFC – 330' aal) to the SW of main runway
Hot Air Balloon launching south of main runway.
Avoid overflying the village of Vimory (0·8 nm South of airfield.
Airfield subject to waterlogging in rainy periods, check by phone before departure.

Fuel: 100LL. Sat, Sun & PHs 0900-1800. Cash only.	**Tel:** 38 85 03 90

Intentionally Blank

N4820·52 E00247·97	**MORET (Episy)**		253 ft AMSL

2 nm SSW of Moret.	**MEL** 109·80 186 07. **BRY** 114·10 262 20
	PTV 116·50 066 24. **TRO** 116·00 279 47

No Radio.
FIS – Paris Information 126·10.

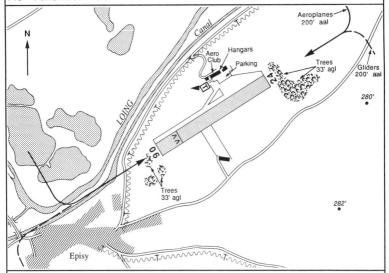

Rwy	Dim(m)	Surface	TORA(m)	LDA(m)	Lighting
06/24	825x100	Grass	06-825	06-675	Nil.
			24-825	24-825	Nil.

Op hrs: HJ except Tue.

Met: Paris (Le Bourget) (1) 48 35 99 98.   **AIS:** Paris NOTAM Office (1) 69 84 56 22

Customs: Nil.

Restaurant: Nil.   **Hangarage:** On request to Aero Club.   **Maintenance:** Nil.

Remarks: Airfield situated beneath Paris TMA 7 (base 3500' ALT).
Microlights prohibited.
Circuits at 700' aal; LH on 06, RH on 24. Glider circuits RH on 06, LH on 24.
Avoid overflying the villages of EPISY, SORQUES and ECUELLES which are within the circuit area.
With wind less than, 4 kt use Rwy 06.
Dep Rwy 24 – turn right 20° as soon as possible after take-off and climb out on heading 260°M.

Fuel: 100LL (except Tue).	**Tel:** 64 45 83 63 A/D and Aero Club.

N4836·08 W00348·90	**MORLAIX (Ploujean)**	282 ft AMSL

1 nm NE of Morlaix.	**QPR 117·80 026 41**
	ARE 112·50 338 18

**Landi APP 122·40, 119·70. Morlaix TWR 118·50. FIS Brest Information 122·80
Lctr 'MLX' 371·0 (226°/2·9 nm to Thr 23). LLZ/DME Rwy 23 (226°M) MX 110·50**

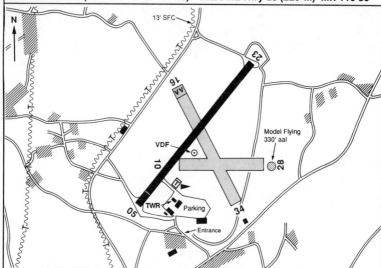

Rwy	Dim(m)	Surface	TORA(m)	LDA(m)	Lighting
05/23	1285x36	Asphalt	05 -1285	05 -1205	Thr Rwy
			23 -1285	23 -1285	Thr Rwy
10/28	610x80	Grass	610	610	Nil
16/34	900x80	Grass	16 -900	16 -850	Nil
			34 -900	34 -900	Nil

Op hrs: Mon-Fri (ex PHs) 0800-1900; Sat, Sun & PHs 0900-1200 & 1400-1900.

Met: Brest (Guipavas) Tel: 98 32 55 53   **AIS:** Brest (Guipavas) Tel: 98 84 60 03

Customs: 12 hrs PNR Mon-Fri 0800-1200 & 1400-1800, other times 24 hrs PNR;
Sat, Sun & PHs on request preceding workday before 1800 hrs — Tel: 98 88 00 36

Restaurant: Bar facilities   **Hangarage:** On request   **Maintenance:** Nil

Remarks: A/D situated beneath Brest CTA (Class **D**) base 1500', see chart opposite.
Circuits at 1000' aal., RH on 34.
Use of Rwy 10/28 prohibited outside ATC Op hrs.
With wind less than 4 kt use Rwy 23.
Surface unusable outside Rwys & Twys.
Microlight activity on SE side of Rwy 05/23.
Model flying up to 330' aal.
Caution. Possible instrument approaches on Rwy 23

Fuel: 100LL, Jet A1. Mon-Fri 0900-1200 & 1400-1800; O/T PNR before 1800 hrs. Sat Sun & PH's O/R preceding Friday before 1800 hrs	**Tel:** 98 88 00 36 Twr. 98 62 16 09 Operator 98 62 16 09 Club. **Telex:** 74696F

Pooley's Flight Guides ©

MORLAIX
VISUAL APP/DEP CHART

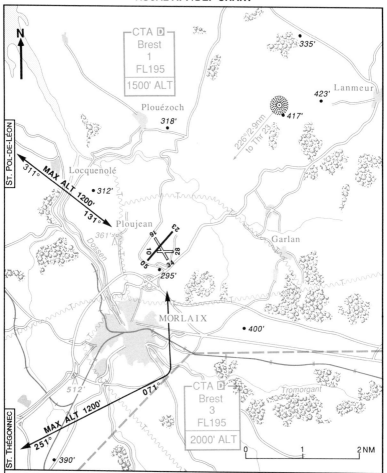

Obtain clearance for Brest CTA from Landi App 122·40 and route as directed or in accordance with the routeings shown above.

Note: Lannion and Dinard TMAs extend to the east from the boundary of the Brest CTA. Lannion App 118·40; Dinard App 120·15

Intentionally Blank

N4832·42 E00032·03	**MORTAGNE-AU-PERCHE**	886 ft AMSL
1 nm NNW of Mortagne	CHW 115·20 285 19.	CDN 116·10 314 45
		DVL 110·20 172 47

No Radio. FIS — Paris Information 129·625.

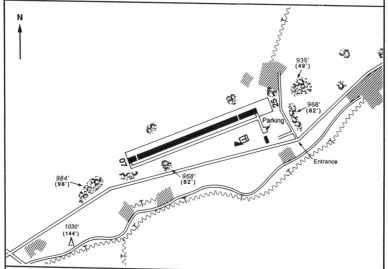

Rwy	Dim(m)	Surface	TORA(m)	LDA(m)	Lighting
07/25	720x20	Asphalt	07 -720	07 -690	Nil
			25 -720	25 -630	Nil

Op hrs: PPR. SR-SS

Met: Alencon (Valframbert) Tel: 33 29 26 96 or Rennes (St.Jacques) Tel: 99 31 91 90.

AIS: Deauville (St. Gatien) Tel: 31 88 31 27.

Customs: Nil

Restaurant: Nil   **Hangarage:** On request   **Maintenance:** Nil

Remarks: Aerodrome is subject to spells of bad weather with very low cloud base.
Visiting pilots are strongly advised to check with the aerodrome by phone before
departure.
Surface unusable outside Rwys, Twys and Aprons.

Fuel: 100LL
O/R Tel: 33 25 20 86.

Tel: 33 25 20 86, 33 25 21 45 or 33 25 18 46

N4709·48 W00136·40	**NANTES (Atlantique)**	89 ft AMSL

4·3 nm SW of Nantes.

Nantes APP 124·90, 121·80. TWR 120·70. ATIS 126·925.
VOR/DME 'NTS' 115·50 (On A/D).   NDB 'GL' 369·0 (032°/6 nm to Thr 03).
ILS Rwy 03 (031°M) NT 109·90.

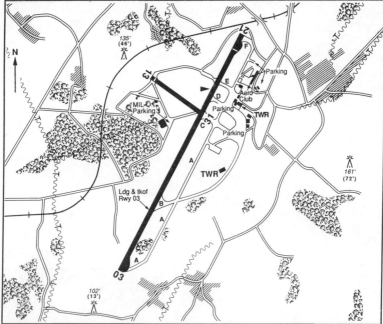

Rwy	Dim(m)	Surface	TORA(m)	LDA(m)	Lighting
03/21	2900x45	Asphalt	03 -2900†	03 -2900†	Ap Thr Rwy
			21 -2900	21 -2695	Thr Rwy PAPI 3°
13/31	650x30	Asphalt	13 -650	13 -590	Nil
			31 -650	31 -650	Nil

† 2000 m take-off & landing for VFR aircraft up to 5700 kg, from abeam Twy A.

Op hrs: H24.

Met: On aerodrome – Tel: 40 84 80 19   **AIS:** On aerodrome

Customs: 0800-2000, other times on prior notice 2 hours before ETA.

Restaurant: Available   **Hangarage:** Nil   **Maintenance:** Limited

Remarks: Circuits at 1000' aal; RH on 21 and 31, LH on 03 and 13.
Gliders prohibited.
Aerobatic Area No. 6380 (6 nm WNW of A/D) 1500' SFC – FL65.
Instrument approaches on Rwy 03.
Unusable outside Rwys & Twys.
Visual APP/DEP Chart — see opposite page

Fuel: 100LL, Jet A1.	**Tel:** 40 84 80 45 ATC. 40 84 80 00 Operator.

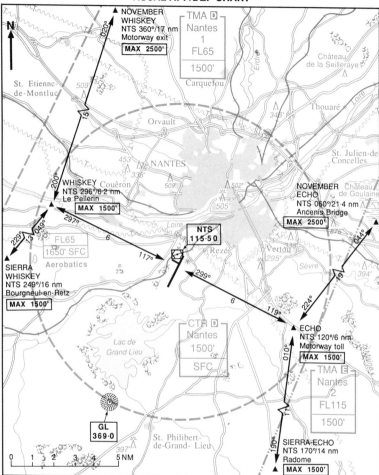

Arrival: Obtain clearance from Nantes APP before reaching the entry points:
NE or NW: Max 2500 ft. **SW, SE, W or E:** Max 1500 ft.
Report 3 mins before reaching these points.
If direct routeing to A/D is authorised avoid overflying the city and outskirts.
Departure: On initial contact with TWR, specify the requested exit point.
Note. Transponder mandatory.

Prior notification is mandatory for SVFR flights and recommended for VFR flights.

Special VFR Minima with IFR Traffic:
<u>Fixed wing:</u> Visibility 5000 m, cloud ceiling 1000 ft.
<u>Helicopters:</u> Visibility 800 m, cloud ceiling 500 ft.

N4700·28 E00306·72	**NEVES (Fourchambault)**	587 ft AMSL
1·5 nm W of Nevers.	NEV 113·40 143 12.	LCA 112·1 067 43
	MOU 116·70 313 28.	ATN 114·90 286 48

Nevers Information 120·60 AFIS. (Air/Air when not manned).
Lctr 'NV' 394·0 (316°/4 nm to Thr 30)

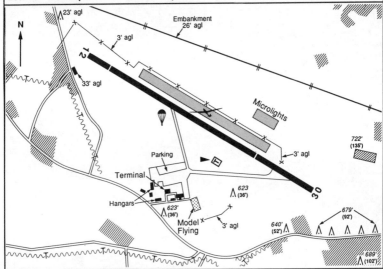

Rwy	Dim(m)	Surface	TORA(m)	LDA(m)	Lighting
12/30	1630x30	Asphalt	12-1630	12-1470	Thr Rwy
			30-1630	30-1240	Thr Rwy PAPI 3·3°
† 12/30	930x60	Grass	12- 930	12- 930	Nil.
			30- 930	30- 930	Nil.

† for use of home based aircraft only.

Op hrs: Mon-Fri 0745-1230 & 1330-1800; Sat 0800-1200 & 1400-1800; Sun PPR
before 1700 hrs Sat; PHs PPR preceding workday before 1700 hrs.

Met: On aerodrome Tel: 86 57 33 19   **AIS:** No provision.

Customs: Mon-Sat (ex PHs) 24 hrs PNR; Sun & PHs 48 hrs PNR.

Restaurant: Nil.   **Hangarage:** Available   **Maintenance:** Nil.

Remarks: Aerodrome situated beneath Restricted Area LF-R20. B2 (base 2500').
Circuits at 1000' aal; RH on 12, LH on 30. Glider operate from Grass Rwy, circuits at
700' aal; LH 0n 12, RH on 30.
Microlights operate from small strip on north side of Grass Rwy.
With wind less than 4 kt, use Rwy 30.
Possible IFR approaches to Asphalt Rwy.
Aerodrome unusable outside Rwys & Twys.

Fuel: 100LL, Jet A1	**Tel:** 86 57 03 92

Intentionally Blank

LFOZ

N4753·92 E00209·92	**ORLEANS (St. Denis de l'Hôtel)**	394 ft AMSL

2·2 nm NE of St. Denis de l'Hôtel.

RBT 114·70 175 46
PTV 116·50 200 06

Bricy APP 122·70. Orleans Information 122·40.
Lctr 'ORS' 322·0 (235°/3·9 nm to Thr 24).

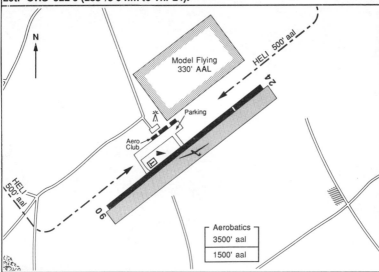

Rwy	Dim(m)	Surface	TORA(m)	LDA(m)	Lighting
06/24	1000x30	Asphalt	06-1000	06-1000	Thr Rwy PAPI 3°
			24-1000	24-820	Thr Rwy PAPI 3°
†06/24	1060x80	Grass	1060	1060	Nil.

† Glider operations only.

Op hrs: Mon-Fri 0800-1200 & 1500-1900; Sat Sun & PHs and O/T PPR preceding workday before 1800 hrs.

Met: Orleans (Bricy) Tel: 38 43 04 00	**AIS:** Orleans (Bricy)	**Customs:** Nil
Restaurant: Nil	**Hangarage:** Nil	**Maintenance:** Limited

Remarks: Aerodrome situated beneath Bretigny CTA (Class **D**) base 4500', and just outside the SE boundary of Orleans CTA (Class **D**) 1500' – 4500'. Entry clearance for Orleans CTA must be obtained from Bricy App.
Circuits at 1000' aal., LH on 06, RH on 24. Glider operations on grass strip with circuits at 660' aal., RH on 06, LH on 24.
Simultaneous use of Asphalt Rwy and grass strip prohibited.
In calm conditions or with crosswinds use Rwy 06.
Para-dropping to south of grass strip.
Possible IFR approaches to Rwy 24.
Aerodrome unusable outside Rwys and Twys.

Fuel: 100LL	**Tel:** 38 59 17 87

N4827·85 W00503·73	**OUESSANT**	138 ft AMSL
1·3 nm E of Lampaul.		**QPR 117·80 317 46**

Ouessant Information 118·10.   FIS Brest Information 122·80.
NDB 'CA' 308·0 (092°/2·6 nm to A/D)

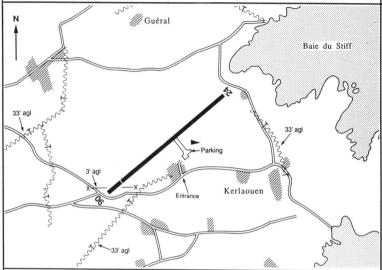

Rwy	Dim(m)	Surface	TORA(m)	LDA(m)	Lighting
06/24	950x25	Asphalt	06 -950	06 -850	Nil
			24 -950	24 -950	Nil

Op hrs: 1 Jun–30 Sep 0800-1200 & 1400-1830;
1 Oct–31 May 0800-0930 & 1600-1730. O/T for public transport & aeromed flights O/R.

Met: Brest (Guipavas) Tel: 98 32 55 53   **AIS:** Brest (Guipavas) Tel: 98 84 61 11

Customs: Nil

Restaurant: Nil   **Hangarage:** Nil   **Maintenance:** Nil

Remarks: Circuits at 700' aal; LH on 24, RH on 06.
Aerodrome surface unusable outside Rwys & Twys.
Flight Plans mandatory.

Fuel: Nil	**Tel:** 98 48 82 09 A/D. 98 84 61 86 Club.

N4850·05 E00216·45	**ISSY-LES-MOULINEAUX "Heliport"**	105 ft AMSL

2·5nm SSW the Arc de Triomphe.	**TSU 108·25 057 08. BT 108·80 223 11**
	PON 111·60 152 18

Moulineaux TWR 118·50
FIS – Paris Information 126·10

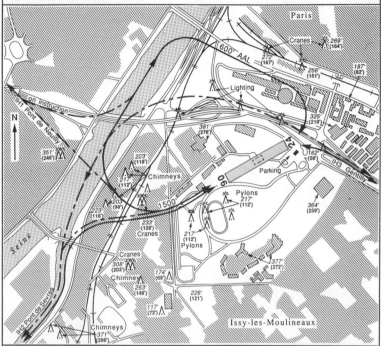

Rwy	Dim(m)	Surface	TORA(m)	LDA(m)	Lighting
06/24	350x50	Grass	—	—	Acceleration/Stop Strip

Op hrs: Mon-Fri 0700-2100, Sat Sun & PHs 0800-2100, SS + 30 latest any day.

Met: Toussus & PARIS (Le Bourget or Orly)   **AIS:** Toussus-le-Noble

Customs: On request. HJ. Tel: (1) 64 46 37 30; Police (1) 45 54 08 76

Accommodation: Available   **Hangarage:** Nil   **Maintenance:** Limited

Remarks: Radio contact mandatory.
Routeing and Procedures — see chart opposite and following page.

The following flights are prohibited:
• School and training flights from or to the heliport;
• non-stop circular flights with passengers from the heliport.

Fuel: Jet A1	**Tel:** (1) 45 54 04 44
PNR from Héli-Union (1) 45 54 92 90	

ISSY-LES-MOULINEAUX – ARR/DEP CHART

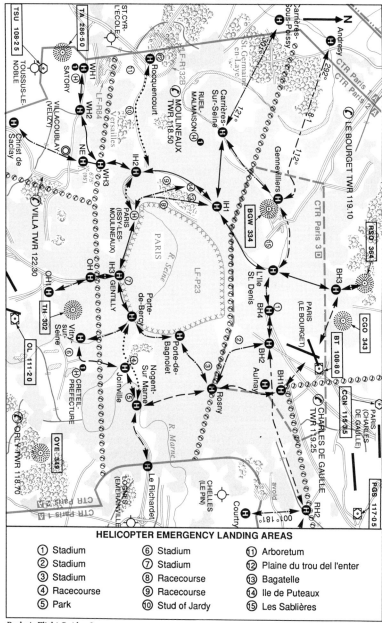

HELICOPTER EMERGENCY LANDING AREAS

① Stadium	⑥ Stadium	⑪ Arboretum
② Stadium	⑦ Stadium	⑫ Plaine du trou del l'enter
③ Stadium	⑧ Racecourse	⑬ Bagatelle
④ Racecourse	⑨ Racecourse	⑭ Ile de Puteaux
⑤ Park	⑩ Stud of Jardy	⑮ Les Sablières

HELICOPTER FLIGHTS WITHIN PARIS CTR 2 & 3

The routes are defined as an exception to 'Overfly Rules' and to rules for Class A Airspace. These routes are compulsory for helicopters flying VFR within the Paris CTR 2 & 3, except for special circumstances specified when necessary by the approach control units of PARIS (Charles-De-Gaulle), PARIS (Orly) or VILLACOUBLAY. In this case, the prescribed 'General Regulations' concerning overflight of PARIS and other built-up areas must be respected in full. Particular conditions concerning use of defined routes may be imposed on helicopter flights by the Director General of Civil Aviation affecting regular flights or particular operations. Use of these routes is limited to daylight hours except as specified overleaf.

SPECIAL CONDITIONS OF USE
Radio contact mandatory: Contact the appropriate ATC authority in compliance with the specified call areas depicted on the chart.

Entry into the traffic circuit of the aerodromes is only permissible via the specified routes.

NIGHT FLIGHT
South Route: (Rocquencourt - Issy-les-Moulineaux - Le Richardet).
Only transport flights, or their positioning flights, are authorized on this route during night periods between 0700 and 2100.

WEATHER MINIMA
Special VFR Minima:
• Visibility: 1500 m;
• Ceiling: 600 ft.

Night Flight Minima:
• Visibility: 8 km;
• Ceiling: 1500 ft.

REMARKS
Flights should be conducted so that the helicopters, taking into account their altitude, will be able to reach an emergency landing point, the Seine or the Marne.

Preferred landing areas for use in emergency are shown on the chart at page 119.

HELICOPTER ROUTES

Route	Description	Altitude (QNH)
SOUTH ROUTE	Motorway A13 between ROCQUENCOURT and Pont de St. Cloud, curve of the Seine to the Heliport; South ring road to PORTE DE BERCY; Motorway A4 to the industrial area LE RICHARDET; then follow the railway to CTR 2 boundary at Villiers-sur-Marne.	1500'
WEST ROUTE	From LUZARCHES follow RN16 then via Lctr 'RSO', avoiding overflying built-up areas. From BH3 to ILE ST. DENIS then follow the Seine to IH2. From IH2 follow RN118 to WH3. From WH3 follow edge of wooded area to WH2. From WH2 follow RN286 to WH1.	1500' 1500' 1000' 1500'
NORTH ROUTE	From the junction of Seine/Oise, fly heading 112°(M) to Lctr 'BGW', around Argenteuil to the North, overflying the railway to the bridge at Gennevilliers; follow the Seine to ILE ST. DENIS, then motorway A1 to industrial area of La Courneuve and the railway between Drancy and RH2; leaving CTR 2 on a heading of 114° (115° PON) to EH3.	1000'
EAST ROUTE	From BH1 follow the motorways; A3 to NOGENT/MARNE, A4 to JOINVILLE-LE-PONT & A86 to VITRY/SEINE. **Note:** This route may be linked with the WEST when authorised by LE BOURGET TOWER.	1500' 1000' or 1300'

Route	Description	Alt. (QNH)
CARRIERES-SOUS-POISSY to PONT DE NEUILLY	Heading121°M between the industrial area North of Poissy, the water tower of Carrières-sur-Seine and the "Ile de Chatou"; rejoin the Seine at IH1.	1500'
ISSY-LES-MOULINEAUX to PONT DE NEUILLY	On instruction from Issy-Les-Moulineaux TWR only, rejoin direct to the Isle of Puteaux above the bridge of Puteaux, overflying the south ring road from the Parc des Princes and the Bois de Boulogne.	1500'
CARRIERES-SUR-SEINE to GENNEVILLIERS	Follow the Seine.	1000' to 1500'
LA COUR NEUVE to ROSNY	Fly around Bobigny overflying the railway.	
MITRY LE NEUF to COURTRY	Heading 181°M to Courtry; to leave CTR 2 to the NE of Chelles Aerodrome. Avoid Chelles traffic circuit.	
ROSNY to VITRY-SUR-SEINE	Follow A3 to porte de BAGNOLET, then West ring road (boulevard périphérique) to PORTE DE BERCY and the Seine to the power station (EDF-GDF) at VITRY-SUR-SEINE.	1500'
GENTILLY to PONDORLY	Follow the motorway A6 to OH1, then to OH2 (Juvisy Railway Station) on clearance from Orly ATC.	
GARE DE JUVISY (railway station) to CROISEMENT A6/N7 (crossroads)	Heading 123°M to SENART SUD; then heading 206°M to YH2 (crossroads A6/N7), and South along the A6 to leave CTR 2. Radio contact with BRETIGNY TWR mandatory.	1000'
PONT DE SEVRES to CHRIST DE SACLAY	From IH2 south along N118 to WH3; then (with clearance from Villacoublay Twr) on heading 208°M overfly Villacoublay to Christ de Saclay.	1500'
CHRIST DE SACLAY to MONTLHERY OUEST	Follow the N118 and the A10 (West) to leave CTR2 at YH1. Obtain clearance from BRETIGNY TWR before entering Bretigny CTR.	1000'

Remarks

- Helicopters may be authorised by ATC to descend to 500' SFC due to weather or traffic conditions.

- The routes detailed above may be used in either direction.

N4858·25 E00226·58	**PARIS (Le Bourget)**	217 ft AMSL

6·5 nm NE of Paris.

De Gaulle APP 121·15, 119·85, 124·35 (Dep). **Le Bourget TWR 119·10, 118·925.**
GND 121·90. ATIS 120·00.   TVOR/DME 'BT' 108·80 (On A/D)
ILS Rwy 07 (071°M) **LBE 109·90. ILS Rwy 25** (*271°M) **LBW 111·10** * LLZ offset 25°

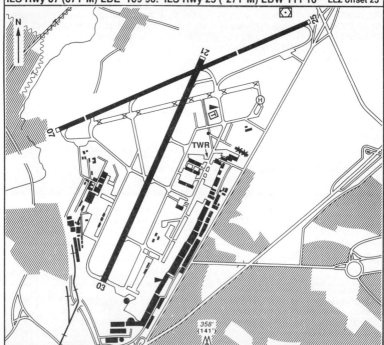

Rwy	Dim(m)	Surface	TORA(m)	LDA(m)	Lighting
03/21	2665x60	Asphalt	03 -2665	03 -2665	Thr Rwy
			21 -2665	21 -2665	Thr Rwy
07/25	3000x45	Asphalt	07 -3000	07 -2700	Ap Thr Rwy
			25 -3000	25 -2100	Thr Rwy

Op hrs: H24

Met: On Aerodrome Tel: (1) 48 35 99 98   **AIS:** On A/D Tel: (1) 48 62 53 14.

Customs: H24

Restaurant: Available   **Hangarage:** Nil   **Maintenance:** Available

Remarks: Prohibited to aircraft not equipped with R/T freqencies for Le Bourget TWR
and De Gaulle APP.
Handling for General Aviation flights must be assured by a based company. Local
training flights PPR. Jet aircraft take-off prohibited 2215-0600 hrs.
See Visual App/Dep Chart & Procedures overleaf.

Fuel: 100LL, Jet A1.	**Tel:** (1) 48 62 53 06 Aerodrome (1) 48 62 53 14 Reporting Office

PARIS (Le Bourget)
VISUAL APP/DEP CHART

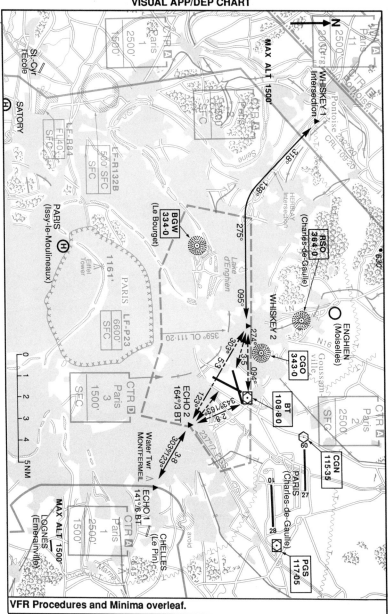

VFR Procedures and Minima overleaf.

PARIS (Le Bourget)
VFR MINIMA & PROCEDURES

Paris CTR Minima:
• **VFR** — Visibility 8 km, ceiling 1500 ft.
• **SVFR** — Visibility 5 km, ceiling 1500 ft.

Le Bourget SVFR Minima
• FIXED WING   Arr/Dep — Visibility 3500 m, ceiling 1500 ft.
• HELICOPTERS   Arr/Dep — Visibility 1500 m, ceiling 600 ft.

Access to/from Le Bourget Airport is via the VFR Transit Route (North):
WHISKEY 1 – LE BOURGET – ECHO 1 (AND VICE VERSA) — see chart opposite.
Use of this route is subject to the following operating restrictions:
• Mandatory Equipment: Suitable radio communications, VOR, Gyro Compass,
  Anti-Collision Light;
• Jet aircraft prohibited;
• Primary Navigation by Visual means, with VOR assistance;
• Max TAS 150 kts;
• Transponder mandatory with high density IFR traffic.

Reporting Points
ECHO 1 — TVOR/DME 'BT' 141°/6 nm (Montfermeil Château)
ECHO 2 — TVOR/DME 'BT' 164°/3 nm (B3 and railway intersection)
WHISKEY 1 — TVOR/DME 'BT' 287°/13 nm (highway intersection)
WHISKEY 2 — TVOR/DME 'BT' 274°/3·5 nm (N1 & N16 junction)

Altitude
The maximum altitude within Paris CTR (Sectors 2 & 3) is 1500'.

Arrival Procedures
Monitor ATIS on 120·00 then request entry clearance from Le Bourget TWR before
reaching the CTR boundary, giving: aircraft registration and type, A/D of departure,
position and altitude.
Entry into Paris CTR Sectors 2 & 3 will be via one of the following entry points:
• Northwest entry — WHISKEY 1 (W1)
• Southeast entry — ECHO 1 (E1)

Routeing
• <u>Northwest Entry</u> — from W1 maintain R 137° "PON" (for approx 5 nm) to intercept
R 274° "BT", maintain R 274° to W2 and proceed as directed.
• <u>Southeast Entry</u> — from E1 maintain R 123° "PON" (for approx 3·5 nm) to E2 and
  proceed as directed.
Note 1. Crossing the centreline of LE BOURGET runways must be carried out overhead the threshold of the runway in use.
Note 2. Transit Route (North) — ATC clearance must be obtained for routeing direct
WHISKEY 2 – ECHO 2 (and vice versa).

Departure Procedures
Specify the required departure route on initial contact with Tower.
Dep Rwy 03: Left or right turn out before reaching the end of the runway.
Dep Rwy 07: Right turn out before reaching the end the runway.
Leave the CTR via Whiskey 2 and Whiskey 1 or ECHO 2 and ECHO 1, advise Le
Bourget TWR on leaving the Area.
Avoid overflying GERGY-PONTOISE (2 nm NW of W1)

Holding — Unless otherwise instructed holding will be carried out overhead
WHISKEY 1 or ECHO 1.

Radio Failure Procedures
• Entry clearance not received or acknowledged:- Do not enter the CTR.
• Entry clearance received and acknowledged:- Proceed in accordance with
acknowledged clearance and hold over Le Bourget Twr. Landing clearance will be
given by green light signals and runway in use will be indicated by the landing 'T'.
• Prior to take-off:- Do not take-off.
• After take-off:- Proceed in accordance with acknowledged clearance.

N4952·18 E00301·77	**PERONNE (St. Quentin)**	292 ft AMSL
5 nm SE of Péronne	**CMB 112·60 196 22. MTD 113·65 050 29**	
	ABB 116·60 113 49	

Péronne Information 128·50. FIS — Paris Information 125·70
Lctr 'PM' 382·0 (274°/3·7 nm to 27 Thr)

Rwy	Dim(m)	Surface	TORA(m)	LDA(m)	Lighting
09/27	2440x45	Asphalt	09 -2440	09 -2440	Thr Rwy
			27 -2440	27 -2225	Thr Rwy

Op hrs: SUMMER Tue-Sat 0830-1200 & 1330-1900.
WINTER Tue-Sat 0830-1200 & 1400-1730.

Met: Lille (Lesquin) Tel: 20 87 51 39.   **AIS:** Lille (Lesquin) Tel: 20 87 52 10.

Customs: Nil

Restaurant: Available. **Hangarage:** Available.   **Maintenance:** Tel: 22 85 68 97

Remarks: Circuits at 1000' aal., LH on 09, RH 0n 27.
Avoid overflying local habitation.
Possible instrument approaches on Rwy 27.
Aerodrome surface unusable outside Rwys & Twys.
Free-Fall Parachuting south of runway up to FL125.

Fuel: 100LL   **Tel:** 22 85 60 34 A/D. 22 84 19 30 Operator

N4910·02 E00218·47	**PERSAN-BEAUMONT**	148 ft AMSL

1·6 nm NE of Beaumont.	PON 111·60 072 12. BVS 115·90 163 17
	MTD 113·65 200 23. CTL 117.60 275 49

Paris Control 124·85, 129·35, 131·35. FIS — Paris Information 125·70.
Creil TWR 120·10. Persan-Beaumont 119·40 (Auto Info)

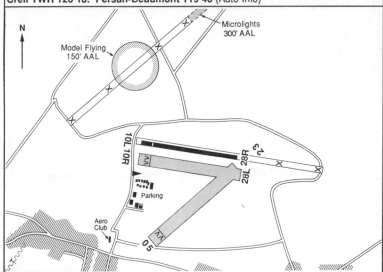

Rwy	Dim(m)	Surface	TORA(m)	LDA(m)	Lighting
05/23	975x100	Grass	05 -975	05 -875	Nil
			23 -975	23 -975	Nil
10L/28R	830x20	Asphalt	10L-830	10L-750	Nil
			28R-830	28R-830	Nil
10R/28L	880x90	Grass	10R-880	10R-755	Nil
			28L-880	28L- 880	Nil

Op hrs: 0900-1200 & 1330-SS plus 30 mins.

Met: Paris (Le Bourget) Tel: 48 35 99 98   **AIS:** Paris (Le Bourget) Tel: 48 62 53 14

Customs: Nil

Restaurant: Nil	**Hangarage:** Nil	**Maintenance:** Limited

Remarks: A/D situated beneath Creil CTR (Class **A**) 1200'–2500'.
Circuits at 660' aal. Circuit pattern as shown on chart opposite.
Aircraft in the circuit pattern for Rwy 05/23 are to remain on north side of River Oise.
Microlight activity up to 330' aal., and model flying up to 150' aal., from the disused
runway 0.5 nm NW of aerodrome.

Visual APP/DEP Chart — opposite.

Fuel: 100LL (HJ except Tues)	**Tel:** (1) 44 70 01 76 A/D. (1) 48 84 43 95 Operator

PERSAN-BEAUMONT
VISUAL APP/DEP CHART

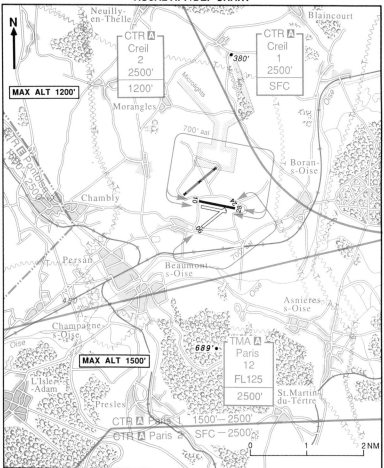

Aerodrome situated beneath Creil CTR (base 1200' ALT).
Compulsory Transit Route — When Creil airbase is active, aircraft may transit CTR Sector 2 only via the compulsory transit route at 1000' MAX ALT:
Follow Auto-route A1 from abeam COMPEIGNE to SENLIS (as depicted on French 1/2 Mil Topo Charts 941 and 942).
Alternative Routeing— via PONTOISE with CTR clearance from Pontoise App 118·80. MAX ALT within Pontoise CTR 2000' and 1200' within Creil CTR.

When Creil airbase is inactive, the Creil CTR may be transitted without restriction by VFR flights up to 2500' ALT.
Contact De Gaulle Approach for information on the activity status of Creil airbase.

LFRP

4·3 nm NNE of Ploërmel.	**DIN 114·30 203 37**	
	RNE 112·80 265 26	

No Radio. FIS — Brest Information 122·80.
Armor 124·725 (VFR clearance for LF-R146)

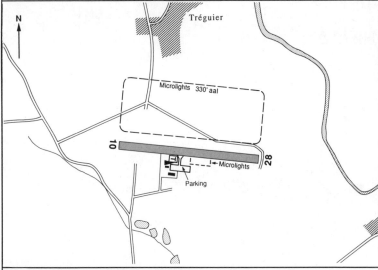

Rwy	Dim(m)	Surface	TORA(m)	LDA(m)	Lighting
10/28	855x60	Grass	10 -855	10 -855	Nil
			28 -855	28 -855	Nil

Op hrs: On request SR-SS.

Met: Rennes (St. Jacques) Tel: 99 31 91 90   **AIS:** Rennes   99 31 31 55

Customs: Nil

Restaurant: Nil   **Hangarage:** Nil   **Maintenance:** Nil

Remarks: Airfield situated beneath Restricted Area LF-R146 (base FL45), activity state from Brest FIS; entry clearance from Armor (Mil) 124·725.
Possible restrictions subject to weather conditions, check by phone prior to departure.
Parachuting on airfield. Avoid overflying LOYAT to south of airfield
Circuits at 1000' aal; LH on 28, RH on 10. With wind less than 4 kt use Rwy 28.
Winch launching from northern side of runway. Gliders circuits at 660' aal; LH on 10, RH on 28.
Microlights — ARR/DEP of microlights overhead runway at 500' aal; circuits to north at 330' aal. Prohibited during parachuting. Overflight of LOYAT prohibited.
With ARR/DEP of aircraft or gliders, microlights must clear runway and remain in parking area or hold in microlight circuit.

Fuel: Nil   **Tel:** 97 74 21 72

N4803·47 W00255·35	**PONTIVY**	407 ft AMSL

1·6 nm ESE of Pontivy.	**DIN 114·30 231 46. QPR 117·80 089 50**
	ARE 112·5 126 32. RNE 112·80 274 47

No Radio. FIS — Brest Information 122·80. Lann-Bihoué TWR 122·70
Armor 125·60 (VFR clearance for LF-R146).

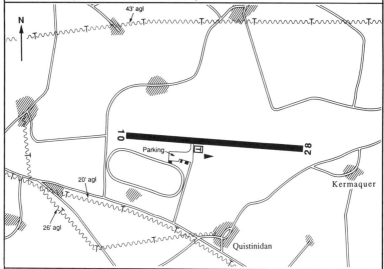

Rwy	Dim(m)	Surface	TORA(m)	LDA(m)	Lighting
10/28	710x60	Grass	10 -1120	10 -1120	Nil.
			28 -1120	28 -1120	Nil.

Op hrs: On request SR-SS daily except Friday.

Met: Rennes (St. Jacques) Tel: 99 31 91 90 **AIS:** Rennes (St. Jacques) 99 31 31 55

Customs: Nil

Restaurant: Club facilities **Hangarage:** On request **Maintenance:** Nil

Remarks: LF-R146 (base FL45) 3·5 nm to NE of airfield, VFR clearance from Amor (Mil).
Lorient CTR (base 1000 ft) 2·5 nm to W and SW, clearance from Lann-Bihoué Twr.

Circuits LH at 1000' aal.
Possible restrictions subject to weather conditions, check by phone prior to departure.
With wind less than 4 kt, use Rwy 10
Mast 965' amsl 558' agl 4 nm WNW of airfield.

Fuel: Nil	**Tel:** 97 25 03 90. **Fax:** 97 25 63 69

N4905·80 E00202·52	**PONTOISE**	325 ft AMSL

3·8 nm NW of Pontoise.

Paris Control 124·85. **Pontoise APP** 118·80. **TWR** 121·20, 119·70. **GND** 121·20.
ATIS 124·125. **VOR 'PON'** 111·60 (On A/D).
ILS Rwy 05 (048°M) CVN 108·10.

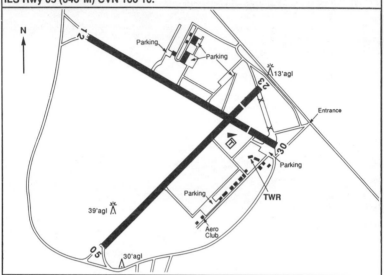

Rwy	Dim(m)	Surface	TORA(m)	LDA(m)	Lighting
05/23	1690x50	Asphalt	05 -1510	05 -1690	Ap Thr Rwy
			23 -1690	23 -1510	Thr Rwy PAPI 3·25°
12/30	1650x50	Asphalt	12 -1410	12 -1650	Nil
			30 -1650	30 -1490	Nil
					IBn 'Q'

Op hrs: ATS 0700-2230, other times on request before 1900 hrs.
Reporting Office & AIS Mon-Fri 0900-1200 & 1330-1800.

Met: On aerodrome Tel: (1) 30 31 03 82   **AIS:** On aerodrome

Customs: Tue-Sat 24hrs PNR; other times PNR previous work day before 1800 hrs.

Restaurant: Available   **Hangarage:** On request   **Maintenance:** Available

Remarks: Non radio aircraft strictly PPR from Tower.
Aerodrome restricted to MTWA 17 tonnes & 25 seats.
Adhere strictly to circuit patterns shown overleaf.
Circuit height: Rwy 05/23 — 1000' aal; Rwy 12/30 — 660' aal; Helicopters — 500' aal.
Circuit direction: LH on 05 and 12, RH on 23 and 30;
Local helicopter flights prohibited, except for locally based aircraft.
Aerodrome surface unusable outside Rwys & Twys.

Visual APP/DEP Chart opposite.

† PPR Aigle Azur Tel: (1) 30313051

Fuel: † North Area 100LL, Jet A1. South Area 100LL.	**Tel:** (1) 30 31 23 08, 30 31 03 82

PONTOISE
VISUAL APP/DEP CHART

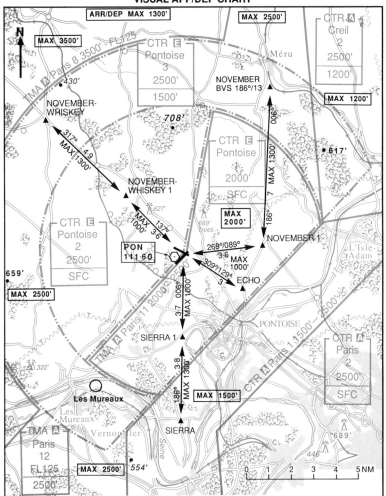

The routes depicted above are mandatory for Special VFR flights and strongly recommended for VFR flights.

Clearance for Paris TMA from Paris Control 124·85.

Contact Pontoise APP 118·80 before entering Pontoise CTR.

Max Alt on Arr/Dep Routes as shown above.

SVFR Minima

With instrument traffic – Visibility 3 km

PONTOISE
CIRCUIT PATTERNS

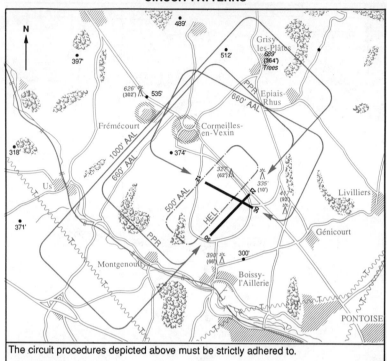

The circuit procedures depicted above must be strictly adhered to.

Pooley's Flight Guides ©

N4728·93 W00306·00	**QUIBERON**	36 ft AMSL
0·8 nm E of Quiberon.		**QPR 117·80 128 52**

Lann-Bihoué APP 123·00 (clearance for Lorient CTA)
Quiberon Information 119·60 Available last Sat/Sun in June to last Sat/Sun in Sep
0930-1230 & 1530-1930 daily except Wed. Air/Air facility outside these times.

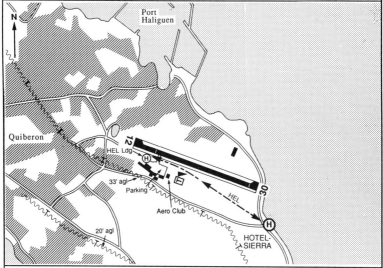

Rwy	Dim(m)	Surface	TORA(m)	LDA(m)	Lighting
12/30	800x25	Asphalt	12 -800	12 -650	Nil
			30 -800	30 -750	Nil

Op hrs: On request SR-SS.

Met: Lorient (Lann-Bihoué) Tel: 97 05 31 72	**AIS:** BTIV Brest Tel: 98 31 84 36

Customs: Nil

Restaurant: Available	**Hangarage:** On request	**Maintenance:** Limited

Remarks: Aerodrome situated beneath Lorient CTA (Class **D**) base 3000', CTA
clearance from Lann-Bihoue App 123·00.
Arrivals from the south, with LF-D13B <u>active</u>, are to route: BELLE-ILE – PHARE DE LA
TEIGNOUSE Lighthouse (2·3 nm SE of Airfield), 045°/225° 10 nm, MAX ALT 3000'.
With LF-D13B <u>inactive</u>, route direct Belle-Ile – Quiberon, 029°/209° 10 nm, MAX ALT
3000'.
Aerodrome surface unusable outside Rwys & Twys.

Helicopters — Arr & Dep via point HOTEL-SIERRA to/from the alighting area. Helicopter
pilots are responsible for maintaining adequate separation from fixed wing traffic using
the runway and must avoid overflying parked aircraft.

Fuel: 100LL. 0930-1200 & 1330-1715 except Wednesdays.	**Tel:** 97 50 11 05 A/D 97 21 00 46 Operator.

N4758·55 W00410·00	QUIMPER (Pluguffan)	302 ft AMSL

2·9 nm SW of Quimper

Quimper APP/TWR 118·30.   FIS — Brest Information 122·80.
VOR/DME 'QPR' 117·80 (045°/1 nm to A/D).
Lctr 'RQ' 380·0 (278°/6·4 nm to Thr 28).   ILS Rwy 28 (278°) QR 110·30

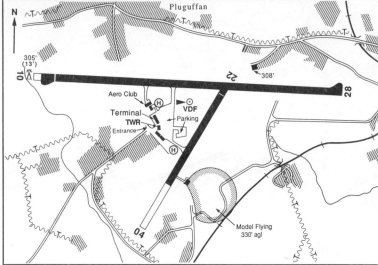

Rwy	Dim(m)	Surface	TORA(m)	LDA(m)	Lighting
10/28	2150x45	Asphalt	10 -2150	10 -2045	Thr Rwy PAPI
			28 -2150	28 -2150	Thr Rwy
04/22	810x45	Asphalt	04 -810	04 -810	Nil
			22 -810	22 -730	Nil

Op hrs: Mon-Fri 0630-2245, Sat 0700-1900, Sun 0900-1100 & 1400-2245; outside these hours AFIS available for commercial flights on 24 hrs PPR.

Met: On aerodrome Tel: 98 94 03 43   **AIS:** On aerodrome

Customs: 2 hours PNR Tel: 99 65 91 68 or LFRQZPZX

Restaurant: Available   **Hangarage:** Nil   **Maintenance:** Nil

Remarks: Quimper CTR (Class **E**) SFC –1500'; TMA (Class **E**) 1500' – FL85, see Visual APP/DEP Chart opposite.
Non radio aircraft prohibited.
Circuits at 1000' aal; LH on 22 and 28, RH on 04 and 10.
Caution: Possible instrument approaches to Rwys 22 and 28.

Note: Prior notification is mandatory for SVFR flights and recommended for VFR flights.

† Fuel availability: Mon-Fri 0800-1900; Sat 0800-1230 Sun 1530-1900; PHs for commercial flights only. Other times 24 hrs PNR Tel: 98 94 30 30.

Fuel: † 100LL, Jet A1	**Tel:** 98 94 01 15 A/D. 98 94 05 22 Aero Club **Fax:** 98 94 02 01

QUIMPER
VISUAL APP/DEP CHART

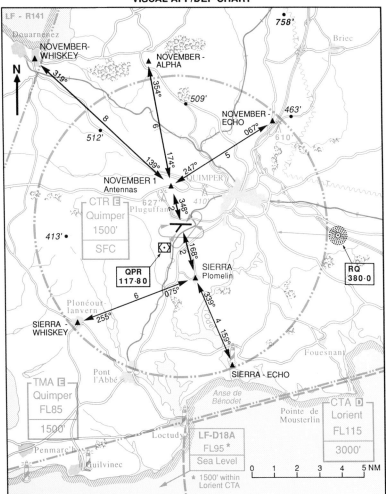

Obtain CTR clearance from TWR 5 mins before ETA for initial entry point.

Special VFR Minima with IFR traffic within CTR
- Fixed Wing: Visibility 5000 m, ceiling 1000'
- Helicopters: Visibility 800 m, ceiling 500'

Radio Failure
- before entry clearance acknowledged: Do not enter CTR
- after entry clearance acknowledged : Proceed in accordance with clearance.

Intentionally Blank

N4741·97 W00202·20	**REDON (Bains-sur-Oust)**	223 ft AMSL
3·5 nm NE of Redon		**NTS 115·50 336 37**
		RNE 112·80 212 26

No Radio. FIS — Brest Information 122·80

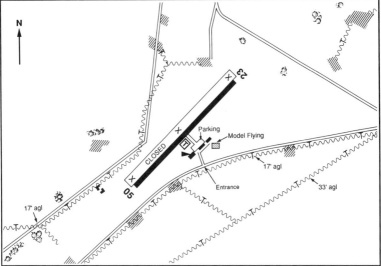

Rwy	Dim(m)	Surface	TORA(m)	LDA(m)	Lighting
05/23	840x20	Asphalt	05 -840	05 -840	Nil
			23 -840	23 -840	Nil

Op hrs: On request SR-SS.

Met: Rennes (St. Jacques) Tel: 99 31 91 90   **AIS:** Rennes Tel: 99 31 31 55

Customs: Nil

Restaurant: Nil   **Hangarage:** On request   **Maintenance:** Nil

Remarks: Circuits at 500' aal; LH on 05, RH on 23.
With wind less than 4 kts, use Rwy 05.
Airfield unusable outside Rwys & Twys.

Fuel: 100LL	**Tel:** 99 71 00 59
Daily 0900-1200 & 1400-1800.	

N4804·35 W00143·77	**RENNES (St Jacques)**	121 ft AMSL

3·2 nm SW of Rennes.

Rennes APP 124·80. TWR 120·50, 119·7.   ATIS 127·875
VOR 'RNE' 112·80 (On A/D). Lctr 'RS' 349·0 (286°/5·45 nm to Thr 29).
ILS Rwy 29 (286°) RS 110·10.

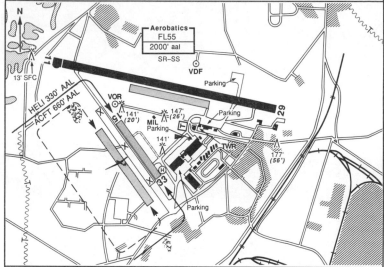

Rwy	Dim(m)	Surface	TORA(m)	LDA(m)	Lighting
11/29	2100x45	Asphalt	11 -2100	11 -2030	Thr Rwy PAPI 3°
			29 -2100	29 -2100	Ap Thr Rwy
11/29	770x80	Grass	770	770	Nil
15/33	650x80	Grass	650	650	Nil
15/33	800x80	Grass	Gliders Only		

Op hrs: H24.

Met: On aerodrome – Tel: 99 31 91 90/99 31 00 88.   **AIS:** On aerodrome

Customs: Mon-Sat except PHs 0700-2130; Sun & PHs 0800-1900. Other times
24hrs PNR on preceding workday before 1700 hrs. Tel: 99650199

Restaurant: Available   **Hangarage:** On request   **Maintenance:** Available

Remarks: Non radio aircraft prohibited.
Circuits: Rwys 11/29 Asphalt & Grass — LH on 11, RH on 29, at 1000' aal.
        Rwy 15/33 — LH on 33, RH on 15, at 660' aal (Helicopters at 330' aal).
Asphalt Rwy 15/33 disused.
Simultaneous use of parallel runways prohibited.
Aerodrome unusable outside Rwys & Twys.
Aerobatics Area (2000' aal – FL55) north of main runway.

Visual APP/DEP Chart — see opposite page.

Fuel: 100LL, Jet A1.	**Tel:** 99 31 31 55 or 99 31 92 89

RENNES (St. Jacques)
VISUAL APP/DEP CHART

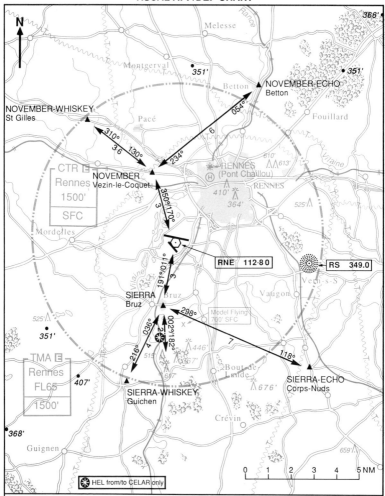

Routes shown above are mandatory for Special VFR flights and recommended for VFR flights — also applicable to helicopter flights.

Special VFR Minima with IFR traffic within CTR
Fixed Wing: Visibility 5000 m, ceiling 1000'.
Helicopters: Visibility 1000 m, ceiling 500'.

N4719·25 E00141·33	**ROMORANTIN (Pruniers)**		289 ft AMSL
3·5nm SW of Romorantin	**AMB** 113·70 106 26.	**BRG**	110·40 310 30
		NEV	113·40 284 52

TWR 118·625 (Availability by NOTAM).
NDB 'RTN' 301·0 (On A/D).

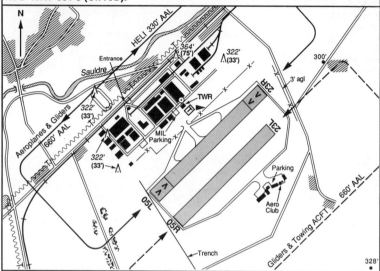

Rwy	Dim(m)	Surface	TORA(m)	LDA(m)	Lighting
05L/23R	800x100	Grass	05L- 800	05L- 800	Nil.
			23R -800	23R-800	Nil.
* 05R/23L	950x100	†Grass/	05R -950	23L -950	Nil.
		Asphalt	23L -950	23L -950	Nil.

† 23L has inset of 520x10m Asphalt strip.

* 05R/23L reserved for home based aircraft and glider operations.

Op hrs: HJ - O/R.

Met: on A/D Tel: 74 76 04 60	**AIS:** Tours (St. Symphorien). 47 54 02 81.

Customs: Nil.

Restaurant: Nil.	**Hangarage:** Nil.	**Maintenance:** Nil.

Remarks: Military aerdrome situated within Restricted Area LF-R19 (SFC – FL45); activity status from Avord App 119·70, entry clearance from Romorantin Twr.
Possible restrictions subject to weather conditions, check by phone prior to departure.
Circuits at 700' aal; LH on 05L and 23L, RH on 05R and 23R.
Rwy 05L/23R - Aeroplanes operate from southern half width, gliders on northern half.
Simultaneous use by aeroplanes and gliders prohibited.
Aerodrome surface unusable outside Rwys & Twys.
Caution: Intensive military flying training traffic and glider activity.

Visual APP/DEP Chart – see opposite.

Fuel: 100LL	**Tel:** 54 76 04 60 - Mil.
	54 96 35 07 - Club.

ROMORANTIN VISUAL APP/DEP CHART

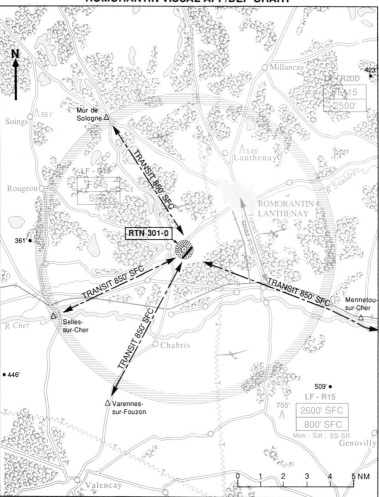

Obtain clearance from Twr before entering LF-R19.
App/Dep via routes shown above at 800' agl; unless otherwise directed by ATC.

Caution: Intense military aircraft activity in the area.

N4923·52 E00111·12	**ROUEN (Boos)**	512 ft AMSL

4·8 nm SE of Rouen.

DPE 115·80 183 32
BVS 115·90 269 38

Rouen APP/TWR 120·20
TVOR 'ROU' 116·80 (224°/6·5 nm to Thr 23). ILS Rwy 23 (225°) RN 110·50.

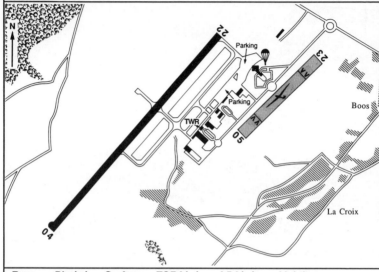

Rwy	Dim(m)	Surface	TORA(m)	LDA(m)	Lighting
04/22	1700x45	Asphalt	04 -1700	04 -1700	Thr Rwy
			22 -1700	22 -1700	Ap Thr Rwy PAPI 3°
05/23	720x80	Grass	Home based gliders only.		Nil.

Op hrs: Mon-Fri 0600-2200; Sat, Sun & PHs 0930-1200 & 1400-1900. O/T PNR.

Met: On aerodrome – Tel: 35794145.   **AIS:** On aerodrome

Customs: HJ. On request before 1000 hrs for clearance same day after 1400 hrs.
On request preceding day before 1800 hrs for clearance next day before 1400 hrs.
Tel: 35 79 41 03/35 79 41 14 or Telex: 180447F.

Restaurant: Available 35 80 22 59 **Hangarage:** On request. **Maintenance:** Limited

Remarks: Rouen CTR (Class **E**) SFC – 2000'; TMA (Class **E**) 3500' ALT – FL115.
See Visual App/Dep Chart opposite.
Simultaneous use of both runways prohibited.
Circuits at 1000', LH on 04, RH on 22. Gliders LH on 23, RH on 05.
Parachuting weekends and PHs, SR-30 to SS+30, MAX FL120.
Aerobatics overhead main runway SR-30 to SS+30 daily, MAX FL120.
Aerodrome surface unusable outside Rwys & Twys.

Fuel: 100LL, Jet A1.	**Tel:** 35 79 41 41 A/D. 35 79 41 50 Twr.
	Fax: 35 80 53 03 A/D. 35 80 48 67 Operator.

ROUEN
VISUAL APP/DEP CHART

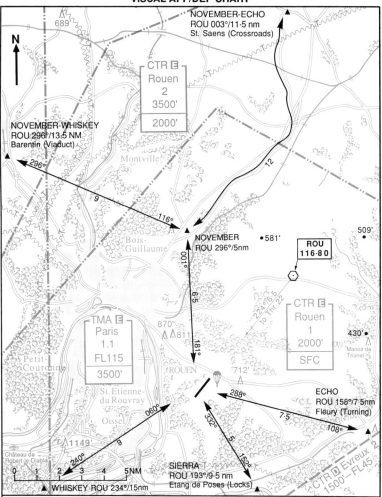

NOVEMBER-ECHO
ROU 003°/11·5 nm
St. Saens (Crossroads)

N

CTR E
Rouen
2
3500'
2000'

NOVEMBER-WHISKEY
ROU 296°/13·5 NM
Barentin (Viaduct)

296°
9
116°

Montville

Bois-Guillaume

NOVEMBER
ROU 296°/5nm

001°
6·5
181°

•581'

ROU
116·80

509'

12

CTR E
Rouen
1
2000'
SFC

430'

Manoir de
Trianel

TMA E
Paris
1.1
FL115
3500'

870'
▲811

Petit
Courronne

ROUEN

St. Etienne-
du Rouvray

Oisse

'712'

288°

332°
5
152°

ECHO
ROU 158°/7·5nm
Fleury (Turning)

7·5
108°

▲1149'

060°
9
240°

Château de
Robert-le-Diable

0 1 2 3 4 5NM

▲ WHISKEY ROU 234°/15nm

SIERRA
ROU 193°/9·5 nm
Etang de Poses (Locks)

CTR D Evreux
1500'–FL45

Obtain entry clearance from Rouen TWR 5 mins before entering CTR via one of the initial reporting points.

Special VFR Minima within CTR

	WITH IFR TRAFFIC	WITHOUT IFR TRAFFIC
Fixed Wing:	Visibility 3000 m, ceiling 1000'	Visibility 1500 m
Helicopters:	Visibility 800 m, ceiling 500'	Visibility 800 m

Intentionally Blank

N4832·32 W00251·32	**ST. BRIEUC (Armor)**	453 ft AMSL

4 nm NW of St. Brieuc.	**DIN 114·30 270 32. ARE 112·50 074 32**
	RNE 112·80 308 53

St. Brieuc TWR 119·40, 119·70. Dinard APP 120·15.
Lctr 'SB' 353·0 (244°/2·8 nm to Thr 24). ILS Rwy 24 (244°) SB 109·30.

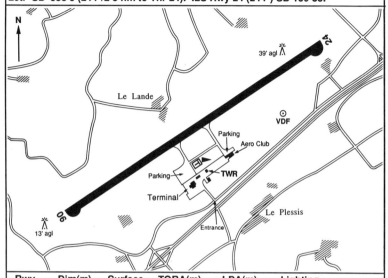

Rwy	Dim(m)	Surface	TORA(m)	LDA(m)	Lighting
06/24	2200x45	Asphalt	06 -2200	06 -2200	Thr Rwy PAPI 3°
			24 -2200	24 -2200	Thr Rwy

Op hrs: Mon-Fri 0530-2230; Sat, Sun & PHs 0800-1200 & 1400-1900. O/T PPR.

Met: On aerodrome Tel: 96 94 94 09.   **AIS:** On aerodrome.

Customs: 1 Apr-31 Oct 0730-2000 O/T O/R. 1 Nov-31 Mar O/R Tel: 99 65 01 99

Restaurant: Nil   **Hangarage:** Nil   **Maintenance:** Limited

Remarks: Aerodrome situated beneath Dinard TMA (Class **E)** 2500' – FL55. TMA clearance from Dinard App.
Aerodrome not available to aircraft without radio.
Circuits at 1000' aal; LH on 06, RH on 24.
With wind less than 4 kt, use Rwy 24.
Airfield surface unusable outside Rwys & Twys.
Caution advised due to possible instrument approaches on Rwy 24.

Fuel: 100LL, Jet A1	**Tel:** 96 94 94 78 A/D. 96 94 20 94 Operator.
	Fax: 96 94 91 37 A/D.

Pooley's Flight Guides ©

N4718·68 W00209·32	**ST. NAZAIRE (Montoir)**	10 ft AMSL

3·7 nm NE of St. Nazaire. | **NTS 115·50 297 24**

Nantes APP 124·90, 121·80. St. Nazaire TWR 118·95.
Lctr 'MT' 398·0 (259°/3·7 nm to Thr 26). ILS Rwy 26 (259°M) MT 108·50.

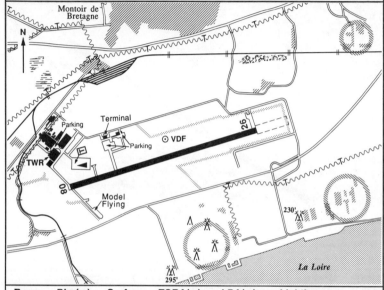

Rwy	Dim(m)	Surface	TORA(m)	LDA(m)	Lighting
08/26	2400x50	Concrete	08 -2400	08 -2400	Thr Rwy
			26 -2400	26 -2400	Thr Rwy

Op hrs: SUMMER Mon-Fri 0800-2000; WINTER Mon-Fri 0800-1830; O/T Mon-Fri O/R
before 1300 hrs, Sat, Sun & PHs O/R preceding workday before 1300 hrs.

Met: On aerodrome Tel: 40 17 13 17   **AIS:** On aerodrome

Customs: Mon-Fri O/R before 1300 hrs; Sat, Sun & PHs O/R preceding workday
before 1200 hrs.

Restaurant: Bar facilities   **Hangarage:** Nil   **Maintenance:** Limited

Remarks: Aerodrome situated beneath Nantes TMA (Class **E**) 1500'–FL115. TMA
clearance from Nantes App 124·90.
Aerodrome not available to non radio aircraft.
Circuits LH, at 1000' aal.
Surface unusable outside Rwys & Twys.
Avoid overflying industrial areas in close proximity to the aerodrome (as shown
above), also areas in the vicinity of the aerodrome as shown opposite.

See Area Chart opposite.

Fuel: Jet A1 (as Op hrs)	**Tel:** 40 90 00 86 A/D. 40 17 13 00 Operator. **Fax:** 40 90 45 68 A/D.

ST. NAZAIRE AREA CHART

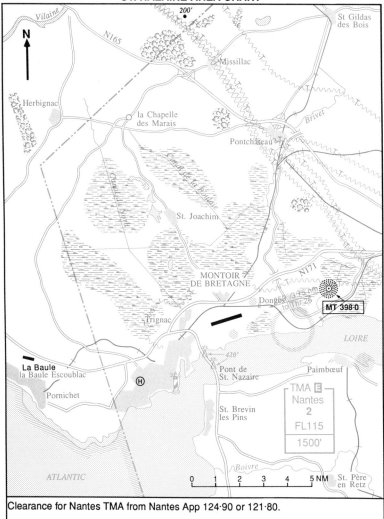

Clearance for Nantes TMA from Nantes App 124·90 or 121·80.

Avoid overflying the following areas in the vicinity of the aerodrome:
ELF Oil Refinery 2·5 nm E of A/D; ELF Gas Storage (*N bank of Loire*) 3 nm E of A/D;
OCTEL KULHMANN Plant (*S bank of Loire*) 6 nm ESE of A/D.

N5043·77 E00214·15	**ST. OMER (Wizernes)**	249 ft AMSL
1·3 nm SW of St. Omer.	**KOK** 114·50 220 27. **BNE** 113·80 067 14	
	ABB 116·60 026 39. **CMB** 112·60 314 46	

No Radio.
FIS — Paris Information 125·70.

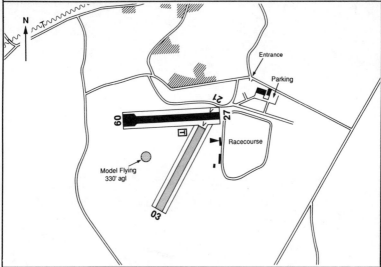

Rwy	Dim(m)	Surface	TORA(m)	LDA(m)	Lighting
03/21	660x60	Grass	03 -660	03 -660	Nil
			21 -660	21 -570	Nil
09/27	570x40	Concrete	09 -570	09 -570	Nil
			27 -570	27 -570	Nil

Op hrs: On request SR–SS.

Met: Le Touquet Tel: 21 05 13 55.   **AIS:** Lille (Lesquin) Tel: 20 87 52 10.

Customs: Nil.

Restaurant: Nil   **Hangarage:** On request   **Maintenance:** Limited.

Remarks: Circuits LH, at 1000' aal.
Parachuting over aerodrome SR–SS, up to FL95.
All aircraft movements prohibited while an aircraft is taxying on the parallel taxiways.
Airfield surface unusable outside Rwys & Twys.

Caution: Racecourse situated on final approach to Rwy 27, expect movement of horses close to Rwy Threshold.

Fuel: 100LL on request HJ.	**Tel:** 21 38 25 42

N4949·02 E00312·40	ST. QUENTIN (Roupy)	325 ft AMSL

2·7 nm WSW of St. Quentin.	CMB 112·60 179 25.	MTD 113·65 064 33
		CTL 117·60 344 43

No Radio.
FIS — Paris Information 125·70.

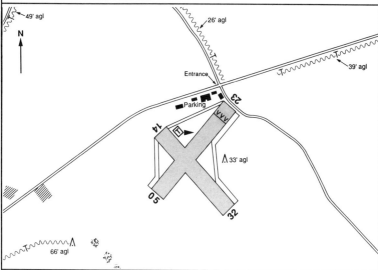

Rwy	Dim(m)	Surface	TORA(m)	LDA(m)	Lighting
05/23	670x100	Grass	05 -670	05 -670	Nil
			23 -670	23 -570	Nil
14/32	620x100	Grass	620	620	Nil

Op hrs: On request SR–SS.

Met: On aerodrome Tel: 23 68 79 28   **AIS:** Lille (Lesquin) Tel: 20 87 52 10

Customs: Nil

Restaurant: Nil   **Hangarage:** Available   **Maintenance:** Nil

Remarks: Circuits at 700' aal (microlights at 350'); LH on 05 and 14, RH on 23 and 32. Glider circuits in opposite direction.
With wind less than 4 kt use Rwy 23.
Use of airfield may be restricted after heavy rainfall or snow, check by phone or by R/T with Beauvais App 119·90.
Microlight activity is restricted to locally based or specially authorised aircraft.

Fuel: MOGAS (HJ except Tues)	**Tel:** 23 68 78 55 or 23 68 70 75 A/D. 23 66 31 59 Aero Club.

N4950·17 E00039·30	**ST. VALERY (Vittefleur)**	272 ft AMSL

3·2 nm SW of St. Valery-en-Caux.

DPE 115·80 259 21
ROU 116·80 316 33

No Radio.
FIS — Paris Information 125·70.

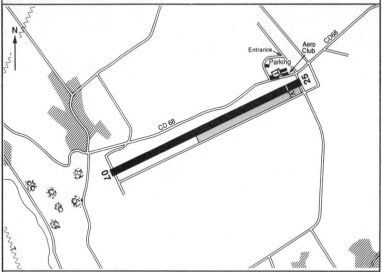

Rwy	Dim(m)	Surface	TORA(m)	LDA(m)	Lighting
07/25	1630x50	Concrete	07 -1630	07 -1630	Nil
			25 -1630	25 -1530	Nil
07/25	900x50	Grass	07 -900	07 -900	Nil
			25 -900	25 -800	Nil

Op hrs: On request SR–SS.

Met: Rouen (Boos) Tel: 35 79 00 50.   **AIS:** Deauville (St. Gatien) Tel: 31 88 31 27.

Customs: Nil

Restaurant: Nil   **Hangarage:** On request   **Maintenance:** Nil

Remarks: Restricted Areas LF-R60A (By NOTAM) and LF-R60B (SFC–3500') are 3 nm
NE of airfield; contact Dieppe Information 119·00 for activity status.
Note. Entry to R60A is prohibited when active.
Circuits LH at 1000' aal. With wind less than 4 kt, use Rwy 25.
Caution: Aircraft taxying to/from the parking area must stop before crossing public
road CD68; vehicles have right of way.
Airfield unusable outside Rwys and Twys.
Warnings:
• Main runway surface rather poor, use by jet aircraft not advisable.
• Airfield is subject to sudden unexpected sea-fog, obtain local MET information and
plan possible diversion to non-coastal aerodrome.

Fuel: 100LL. O/R Aero Club except Tues.	**Tel:** 35 97 10 33

N4715.47 W00006.73	**SAUMUR (St. Florent)**	269 ft AMSL
1·3 nm W of Saumur.	**AMB 113·70 262 48. ANG 113·00 123 35**	
	POI 113·30 341 44	

Saumur Information 120·60.
Lctr 'SR' 372·0 (On A/D).

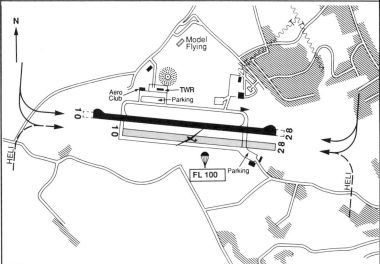

Rwy	Dim(m)	Surface	TORA(m)	LDA(m)	Lighting
10/28	1140x30	Asphalt	10-1140	10-1140	Thr Rwy
			28-1140	28-1140	Thr Rwy
†10/28	970x40	Grass	970	970	Nil

†Runway reserved for home based aircraft only.

Op hrs: 1/4-30/9 0900-1200 & 1400-1800; 1/10-31/3 0900-1130 & 1400-1700 except Wed, Sun & PHs.

Met: Angers Tel: 41 34 32 19	**AIS:** Nantes Tel: 40 84 80 45	**Customs:** Nil
Restaurant: Nil	**Hangarage:** Available	**Maintenance:** Limited

Remarks: Circuits at 1000' aal., LH on 10, RH on 28. Gliders and helicopters LH on 28, RH on 10 on grass runway.
Microlights prohibited.
Simultaneous use of both runways strictly prohibited.
With wind less than 4 kts use Rwy 28.
Airfield unusable outside Rwys & Twys.

Fuel: 100LL	**Tel:** 41 50 65 49

Intentionally Blank

N4657·72 W0009·17	**THOUARS**	341 ft AMSL

2·7 nm ESE of Thouars.	POI 113·30 324 29
	ANG 113·00 145 45

Thouars Auto Information 123·35.
FIS – Bordeaux Information 125·30.

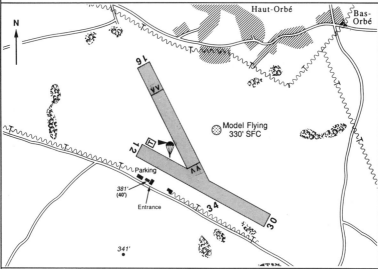

Rwy	Dim(m)	Surface	TORA(m)	LDA(m)	Lighting
12/30	950x100	Grass	12 -950	12 -950	Nil.
			30 -950	30 -950	Nil.
16/34	950x100	Grass	16 -950	16 -725	Nil.
			34 -950	34 -725	Nil.

Op hrs: HJ. O/R

Met: POITIERS (Biard) Tel: 49 58 22 90.   **AIS:** POITIERS (Biard) Tel: 49 58 24 91.

Customs: Nil.

Restaurant: Nil.   **Hangarage:** Nil.   **Maintenance:** Nil.

Remarks: Airfield situated 2 nm North of Restricted Area LF-R149B (800'agl – 1500' agl), penetration prohibited when active. Activity status from Bordeaux Information or on Free-phone 05 24 54 66.
Circuits at 1000' aal; LH on 30 and 34, RH 12 and 16. Gliders at 700' aal.
If wind less than 4 kt, use Rwy 30.
Parachuting at aerodrome SR –SS, 2000 ft or FL110.
Model flying north side of runways, SR – SS, up to 330 ft aal.

Fuel: 100LL	**Tel:** 49 66 21 69.

| N4725·95 E00043·47 | **TOURS (St. Symphorien)** | 354 ft AMSL |

3·2 nm NNE of Tours.

**Tours APP 121·00. TWR/AFIS 118·30. GND 122·10. VDF 118·30, 123·30.
TACAN 'TUR' 113·80 (on A/D). NDB 'TUR' 331·0 (199°/7·7 nm to Thr 20).
ILS Rwy 20 (199°) 'TS' 109·90.**

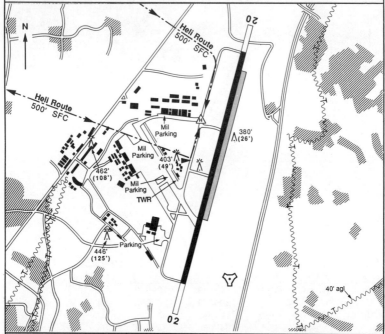

Rwy	Dim(m)	Surface	TORA(m)	LDA(m)	Lighting
02/20	2400x45	Asphalt	02 - 2400	02 - 2400	Thr Rwy VASIS 2·5°
			20 - 2400	20 - 2400	App Thr Rwy VASIS 2·5°

Emergency Grass Strip 02/20, 1500x60m adjacent to the south side of Rwy.

Op hrs: Mon-Fri 0600-2300; Sat, Sat & PHs 0800-1900. O/T PPR.

Met: On A/D Tel: 47 29 19 60.   **AIS:** On Aerodrome.

Customs: 4 hours PNR. Tel: 47 54 63 25

Restaurant: Available   **Hangarage & Maintenance:** Tel: 47 51 25 64.

Remarks: Tours CTR (Class **D**) SFC – 3500'. See Visual App/Dep Chart opposite.
Microlights and gliders prohibited.
Circuits at 700' aal; LH on 20, RH on 02.
Training flights (traffic circuits, touch-and-go and ILS) prohibited outside of ATS
operating hours.
Aerodrome surfaces unusable outside Rwys and Twys.

| **Fuel:**100LL, Jet A1. | **Tel:** 47 54 19 46 (Civ), 47 54 02 81 (Mil). **Fax:** 47 42 59 45 (Civ). |

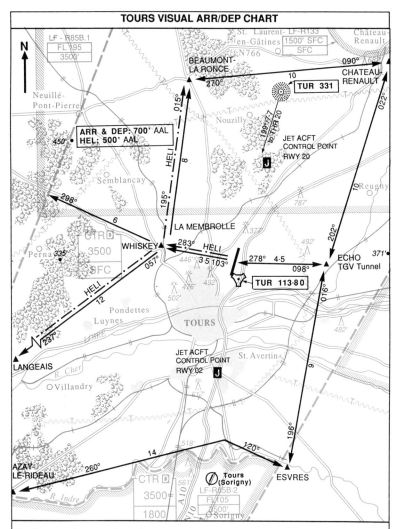

Obtain entry clearance from Tours Twr 118·30 before entering CTR.

SVFR Minima

Propeller Aircraft: Visibility 3 km, ceiling 1000 ft.
Helicopters: Visibility 800 m, ceiling 500 ft.
Jet Aircraft: Visibility 5 km, ceiling 1500 ft.

Procedures — see overleaf.

ARRIVAL, DEPARTURE & TRANSIT PROCEDURES

ATC clearance must be obtained from Tours TWR before entering the CTR.

ARRIVAL PROCEDURES

Fixed Wing

Routes to be flown at 700' aal

From the West :
- Via BEAUMONT LA RONCE to CHATEAUX RENAULT flying south of the N766 in order to avoid LF-R133, then to ECHO (TGV Tunnel); or
- Follow the River Indre towards Esvre then to ECHO.

From the East:
- Via CHATEAUX RENAULT – ECHO;
- Along the River Loire to ECHO;
- Via ESVRES – ECHO.

Helicopters

Routes to be flown at 500' aal.

From the West:
- Via BEAUMONT LA RONCE to WHISKEY (La Menbrolle);
- Via LANGEAS to WHISKEY (La Menbrolle).

From the East: As for Fixed Wing Procedure above.

DEPARTURE PROCEDURES

Fixed Wing & Helicopters

On initial contact with TWR, specify East or West departure.
Fixed Wing at 700' aal; Helicopters at 500' aal.

To the East:
Reverse of East Arrival route, first reporting point ECHO (TGV Tunnel) and comply with ATC instructions.

To the West:
First reporting point WHISKEY (La Menbrolle) and comply with ATC instructions.

TRANSIT PROCEDURES

Fixed Wing at 700' aal; Helicopters at 500' aal.

Recommended Routeing:
- Beaumont La Ronce – Chateau Renault;
- Azay Le Rideau – Esvres;
- Chateau Renault – Esvres.

LFEN

N4716·05 E00042·07	**TOURS (Sorigny)**	299 ft AMSL

7 nm S of Tours.

AMB 113·70	242 18
POI 113·30	026 44

No Radio.
Tours APP 121·00. Tours Airport 118·30.

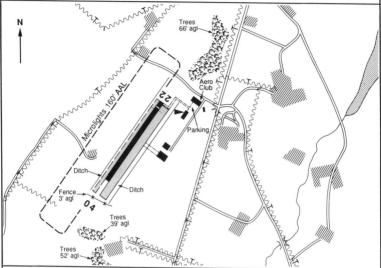

Rwy	Dim(m)	Surface	TORA(m)	LDA(m)	Lighting
04/22	580x18	Asphalt	04 -580	04 -580	Nil
			22 -580	22 -550	Nil
04/22	675x50	Grass	675	675	Nil

Op hrs: On request SR–SS.

Met: Tours (St. Symphorien) Tel: 47 29 19 60 **AIS:** Tours (St. Sym) Tel: 47 54 02 81

Customs: Nil

Restaurant: Nil   **Hangarage:** Nil   **Maintenance:** Limited

Remarks: Airfield situated beneath Tours CTR (Class **D**) 1800'–3500', obtain entry clearance from Tours TWR 118·30. See Tours Visual App/Dep Chart at page 155.
Circuits at 660' aal., LH on 22, RH 0n 04. During calm conditions use Rwy 22.
Home based microlights operate from Grass Strip on West side of Asphalt Rwy, microlight circuits to the West at 160' aal.
Simultaneous use of Asphalt Rwy and Grass Rwy prohibited.
Do not park on Twy in front of 22 Thr.
Caution: Stop and look for traffic on approach to Grass Rwy 22 when taxying to threshold of Asphalt Rwy 22.
Airfield unusable outside Rwys & Twys.

Fuel: 100LL (0900-1200 & 1400-1900, except Tues)	**Tel:** 47 26 01 14 Club. 47 26 22 33 Police.

N4845·05 E00206·78	**TOUSSUS-LE NOBLE**	538 ft AMSL

3·2 nm SSW of Versailles.

Toussus APP 120·75, 119·70. TWR 119·30. GND 121·30. ATIS 127·475.
TVOR 'TSU' 108·25 (On A/D). ILS Rwy 25R (255°M) TNO 109·30.

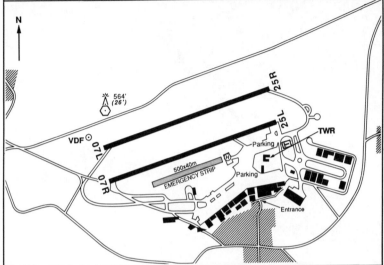

Rwy	Dim(m)	Surface	TORA(m)	LDA(m)	Lighting
07L/25R	1100x30	Asphalt	07L-1100 25R-1100	07L-1100 25R-1100	Thr Rwy VASIS Ap Thr Rwy VASIS
07R/25L	1050	Asphalt	1050	1050	Nil
07/25	500x40	Grass	EMERGENCY STRIP		Nil

Op hrs: 0700-2230 daily.

Met: On aerodrome, Tel: (1)39 56 21 43.	**AIS:** On aerodrome

Customs: 0700-SS+30; SS+30-2230 & 0600-0700 on request 1 hour before SS.

Restaurant: Available	**Hangarage:** On request	**Maintenance:** Available

Remarks: Aerodrome situated beneath Paris CTR 1 (1500' – 2500' ALT) Class A
Controlled Airspace. Specific Arr/Dep Procedures apply — see chart opposite and
Regulations and Procedures at page 160.
Non radio aircraft prohibited.
Circuits at 800' aal; LH on 25, RH on 07. Helicopters circuits inside standard circuit at
600' aal.
Aerodrome surface unusable outside Rwys & Twys.

VFR Flight Plans must include the following addressees: LFPNZPZX & LFPBZPZX.

Fuel: 100LL, Jet A1. 0700-2100 (Winter 2000)	**Tel:** (1) 39 56 51 92 A/D. (1) 48 84 43 95 Operator.

TOUSSUS-LE-NOBLE
VISUAL APP/DEP CHART

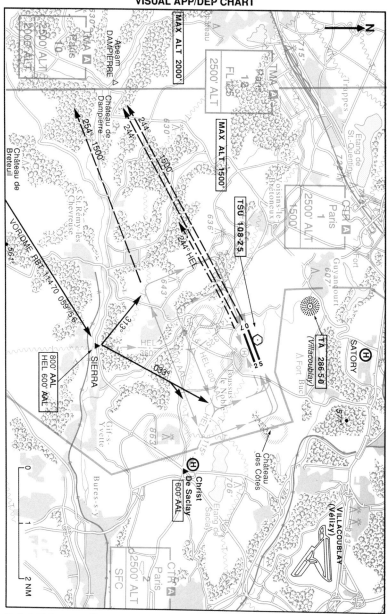

ARRIVALS

Fixed wing

Via the compulsory entry point SIERRA (RBT 114·70 060°/5·6 nm) at 800' SFC.

Helicopters

Via the entry point SIERRA or CHRIST DE SACLAY at 600' SFC.

DEPARTURES

Fixed wing

• Dep 07 — Climb on the outer circuit pattern (see chart page at 159) to 1500' and follow magnetic track 254° to ABEAM DAMPIERRE.

• Dep 25 — After take-off at end of Rwy turn left 10° to magnetic track 244° to ABEAM DAMPIERRE AND CLIMB TO 1500'.

Helicopters

Departure to CHRIST DE SACLAY:

East and West departures — Climb on inner traffic circuit to 600' SFC then proceed to CHRIST DE SACLAY.

Departure to ABEAM DAMPIERRE:

• Departures to the East — Climb on the outer traffic circuit to 1500' and follow magnetic track 254° to ABEAM DAMPIERRE.

• Departures to the West — After take-off, at end of emergency strip, turn left 10°and follow magnetic track 244° to ABEAM DAMPIERRE climbing to 1500'.

Note: Helicopter procedures may be subject to change – check by phone before departure.

N4743·20 W00243·32	**VANNES (Meucon)**	446 ft AMSL

4·3 nm NNE of Vannes.	**RNE 112·80 247 45**
	ARE 112·50 141 51

Vannes TWR 122·60.   FIS — Brest Info 122·80.
Lctr 'VA' 342·50 (225°/3·3 nm to Thr 23).

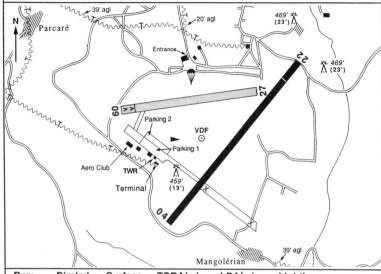

Rwy	Dim(m)	Surface	TORA(m)	LDA(m)	Lighting
04/22	1530x45	Concrete	04 -1530	04 -1530	Thr Rwy PAPI 3°
			22 -1530	22 -1380	Thr Rwy
09/27	1025x60	Grass	09 -1025	09 -935	Nil
			27 -1025	27 -1025	Nil

Op hrs: Mon-Fri 0730-2030; Sat, Sun & PHs 0730-1200 & 1400-2030. O/T PPR.

Met: Rennes (St. Jacques) Tel: 99 31 91 90.   **AIS:** Rennes Tel: 99 31 31 55

Customs: HJ. 24 hrs PNR preceding workday before 1700 hrs.

Restaurant: Nil   **Hangarage:** On request   **Maintenance:** Nil

Remarks: A/D situated 4 nm outside eastern boundary of Lorient CTA (Class **D**)
base 3000'; clearance from Lann-Bihoué App 123·00.
Non radio aircraft prohibited.
Danger Area LF-D573 (SFC–13,120'), 1 nm NW of aerodrome.
Circuits at 1000' aal; LH on 22 and 09, RH on 04 and 27.
With wind less than 4 kt, use Rwy 04.
Aerodrome unusable outside Rwys & Twys.
Possible instrument approaches on Rwy 22.
Parachuting over aerodrome H24, up to FL195.

Fuel: 100LL, Jet A1. (Mon-Fri 09-1200 & 14-1800; Sat, Sun PHs 14-1900)	**Tel:** 97 60 70 52 or 97 60 66 83 Twr **Fax:** 97 44 58 34

Intentionally Blank

N5020·30 E00259·60	**VITRY-EN ARTOIS**	174 ft AMSL

1 nm NNE of Vitry-en-Artois.   **BNE 113·80 116 45.   CMB 112·60 320 09**
                                                        MTD 113·65 026 51

Lille APP 127·90. Vitry-en-Artois Club 123·50

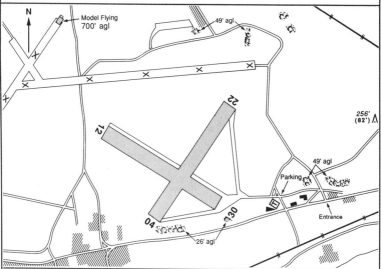

Rwy	Dim(m)	Surface	TORA(m)	LDA(m)	Lighting
12/30	900x100	Grass	900	900	Nil.
04/22	900x100	Grass	900	900	Nil.

Op hrs: On request. HJ.

Met: Lille (Villenueve) Tel: 200 4720 20   **AIS:** Lille (Villenueve) Tel: 20 87 52 10

Customs: Nil.

Restaurant: Nil.   **Hangarage:** Available   **Maintenance:** Nil.

Remarks: Airfield situated beneath LF-R102A.4 (base 1600'), with LF-R102A.1 (SFC – FL45) activity status from Lille App, entry clearance from Cambrai App 132·65.
Circuits left-hand at 1000' aal.
Departure Rwy 22 — turn left after take-off heading 175°M to avoid overflying Vitry-en-Artois.
Take-off/Landing on Rwy 12/30 prohibited if an aircraft is on the adjacent taxiway.
With wind less than 10 kt, use Rwy 12.
Microlight activity on airfield, circuits at 330' aal.
Airfield unusable outside Rwys & Twys.

Fuel: 100LL (except Tue) Cash only.	**Tel:** 21 50 07 75

RESTRICTED AERODROMES

The following aerodromes are not normally available to visiting aircraft. They are notified as being available only to home based aircraft and specified users.
Permission for use may be granted on written application to the appropriate Regional Authority.

ALBERT (Bray)   **LFAQ**   N4958 E00241   377 ft AMSL
Rwy: 10/28 1545 x 50m PSP
Radio: Nil.
Fuel: 80, Jet A1.   **Tel:** 22 75 19 77 Ext 3368

ANCENIS   **LFFI**   N4723·93 W00111·17   95 ft AMSL
1·9 nm N of Ancenis
Rwy: 01/19 800 x 20m Asphalt
Radio: Nil.
Fuel: 100LL.   **Tel:** 40 83 28 14

AVRANCHES (Le Val St. Pere) **LFRW** N4839·72 W00124·20   26 ft AMSL
1·6 nm SW of Avranches
Rwy: 04/22 750 x 60m Grass; 13/31 500 x 60m Grass
Radio: Nil
Fuel: 100LL.   **Tel:** 33 58 02 91

BAILLEAU (Armenonville) LFFL   N4830·95 E00138·40   509 ft AMSL
0·8 nm SSW of Bailleau Armenonville
Rwy: 08/26 780 x 100m Grass; 00/18 780 x 100m Grass
Radio: Auto Information 122·05
Fuel: 100LL.   **Tel:** 37 31 43 74

BEYNES (Thiverval)   **LFPF**   N4850·62 E00154·53   371 ft AMSL
1·3 nm SE of Beynes
Rwy: 12/30 1000 x 80m Grass
Radio: Air to Air 120·425
Fuel: 100LL.   **Tel:** 34 89 10 05

BUNO (Bonnevaux)   **LFFB**   N4821·07 E00225·53   420 ft AMSL
1·6 nm ESE of Buno Bonnevaux
Rwy: 10/28 800 x 100m Asphalt; 02/20 620 x 80m Asphalt
Radio: Air to Air 119·375
Fuel: 100LL.   **Tel:** 64 99 49 41

CONDE-SUR-NOIREAU LFAN   N4853·50 W00030·12   833 ft AMSL
3·2 nm NE of Conde sur Noireau
Rwy: 09/27 700 x 60m Grass
Radio: Nil.
Fuel: 100LL.   **Tel:** 31 69 07 21

DUNKIRK (Ghyvelde)   **LFAK**   N5102·43 E00233·02   3 ft BMSL
6·5 nm SE of Dunkirk
Rwy: 07/25 800 x 45m Grass
Radio: Koksijde App 122·50
Fuel: 100LL.   **Tel:** Club 28 26 88 40

ENGHIEN (Moisselles)   **LFFE**   N4902·78 E00221·18   335 ft AMSL
0·6 nm ESE of Moisselles
Rwy: 07/25 740 x 80m   Grass; 16/34 570 x 80m Grass
Radio: Air to Air 121·25
Fuel: 100LL.   **Tel:** 39 91 05 60

ETREPAGNY   **LFFY**   N4918·37 E00138·32   308 ft AMSL
0·8nm E of Etrepagny
Rwy: 12/30 674 x 95m Grass
Radio: Nil.
Fuel: 100LL.   **Tel:** 32 55 73 29

FALAISE (Monts d'Eraines) LFAS N4855·63 W00008·68 512 ft AMSL
2·7 nm NE of Falaise d'Avallon
Rwy: 06/24 850 x 100m Grass; 01/19 650 x 60m Grass
Radio: Air to Air 123·175
Fuel: 100LL **Tel:** 31 90 06 54

LA FERTE - ALAIS LFFQ N4829·87 E00220·60 453 ft AMSL
1·1 nm NNW of La Ferte Alais
Rwy: 11/29 1000 x 90m Grass
Radio: Nil.
Fuel: 80/87 **Tel:** 1- 64 57 52 89

LAMOTTE - BEUVRON LFFM N4739·40 E00159·35 413 ft AMSL
3·5nm NNW of Lamotte - Beuvron
Rwy: 16/34 570 x 75m Grass
Radio: Nil.
Fuel: Nil. **Tel:** 54 88 02 15

MANTES (Cherence) LFFC N4904·73 E00141·38 512 ft AMSL
5·4 nm NNW of Mantes la Jolie
Rwy: 04/22 900 x 100m Grass; 13/31 900 x 100m Grass
Radio: Air to Air 119·65
Fuel: 100LL. **Tel:** 34 78 13 33

MELUN (Villaroche) LFPM N4836·37 E00240·33 302 ft AMSL
4·6 nm N of Melun
Rwy: 11/29 1975 x 45m Asphalt; 02/20 1300 x 30m Asphalt
Radio: c/s Melun APP 123·20, TWR 121·10, ATIS 128·175
Fuel: 100LL **Tel:** 64 71 44 44

MONTDIDIER LFAR N4940·38 E00234·15 358 ft AMSL
1·3 nm N of Montdidier
Rwy: 09/27 750 x 100m Grass
Radio: Nil.
Fuel: Nil. **Tel:** Club 22 78 82 51

PITHIVIERS LFFP N4809·43 E00211·55 384 ft AMSL
2·2 nm WSW of Pithiviers
Rwy: 07/25 800 x 70m Grass
Radio: Nil.
Fuel: 100LL **Tel:** 38 30 08 27

ST. ANDRE DE L'EURE LFFD N4853·92 E00115·03 489 ft AMSL
1·1 nm SW of St. Andre de l'Eure
Rwy: 06/24 1590 x 60m Asphalt; 06/24 800 x 50m Grass
Radio: Evreux App 123·60
Fuel: Nil. **Tel:** 32 37 24 74

VAUVILLE LFAU N4937·45 W00149·75 456 ft AMSL
0·9 nm SSE of Vauville
Rwy: 15/33 650 x 60m Grass
Radio: Nil.
Fuel: Nil. **Tel:** 33 52 77 72

VIERZON (Merveau) LFFV N4711·68 E00204·00 430 ft AMSL
1·1 nm S of Vierzon
Rwy: 04/22 650 x 100m Grass
Radio: Auto Information 125·25
Fuel: Nil. **Tel:** 48 75 12 87

MILITARY AERODROMES

The following military aerodromes are not normally available for use by civil aircraft except on prior permission. Some of these aerodromes may require written application.

AVORD   **LFOA**   N4703·42 E00238·53   577 ft AMSL
11nm W of Bourges
Rwy: 06/24 3500 x 45m Asphalt; 06/24 560 x 70m Grass
Radio: APP 119·70 TWR 122·10 VDF 119·70
Fuel: 100LL, Jet A1   **Tel:** 48 69 13 05

CREIL   **LFPC**   N4915·13 E00231·37   289 ft AMSL
1·5 nm SE of Creil
Rwy: 07/25 2400 x 50m Concrete
Radio: TWR 119·70, 122·10
Fuel: 100LL, Jet A1   **Tel:** 44 55 03 01

EVREUX (Fauville)   **LFOE**   N4901·73 E00113·27   463 ft AMSL
2·5 nm E of Evreux
Rwy: 04/22 2995 x 45m Asphalt
Radio: APP 123·60, 142·45. TWR 119·70, 122·10
Fuel: 100LL, Jet A1   **Tel:** 32 39 53 81

LANDIVISIAU   **LFRJ**   N4831·82 W00409·05   348 ft AMSL
3 nm NW of Landivisiau
Rwy: 08/26 2700 x 45m Concrete
Radio: c/s Landi APP 122·40, 119·70. TWR 119·70, 119·20
Fuel: 100LL, Jet A1   **Tel:** 98 24 20 20

LANVEOC (Poulmic)   **LFRL**   N4816·92 W00426·75   285 ft AMSL
0·5 nm E of Lanveoc
Rwy: 06/24 1130 x 40m Concrete
Radio: APP 120·60, 119·30. TWR 122·10, 123·20
Fuel: 100LL, Jet A1   **Tel:** 98 23 30 10

LORIENT (Lann-Bihoue) LFRH   N4745·63 W0326·33   161 ft AMSL
2·2 nm WNW of Lorient
Rwy: 02/20 1670 x 45m Concrete; 08/26 2400 x 45m Concrete
Radio: c/s Lann Bihoue APP 123·00,122·30. TWR 122·70. RADAR 119·80
Fuel: 100LL   **Tel:** 97 12 90 00

ORLEANS (Bricy)   **LFOJ**   N4759·20 E00145·72   410 ft AMSL
7 nm NNW of Orleans
Rwy: 07/25 2400 x 45m Concrete
Radio: c/s Bricy APP 138·75, 122·70. TWR 122·70, 122·10
Fuel: 100LL, Jet A1   **Tel:** 38 43 23 60

VILLACOUBLAY (Velizy) LFPV   N4846·48 E00211·55   581 ft AMSL
7 nm NNW of Paris (Orly)
Rwy: 09/27 1800 x 45m Asphalt
Radio: c/s Villa APP 118·05, 142·45. TWR 122·30, 122·10
Fuel: 100LL, Jet A1   **Tel:** (1) 46 30 23 88

CONVERSION TABLES

AVIATION FUEL CONVERSION CHART

Imp Gals	US Galls	Litres	AVGAS Lbs	AVGAS Kgs	AVTUR Lbs	AVTUR Kgs
1	1·2	4·55	7·2	3·3	7·9	3·6
2	2·4	9·1	14·4	6·6	15·8	7·2
3	3·6	13·6	21·6	9·9	23·7	10·8
4	4·8	18·2	28·4	13·2	31·6	14·4
5	6·0	22·8	36	16·5	39·5	18
6	7·2	27·2	43·2	19·8	47·4	21·6
7	8·4	31·8	50·9	23·1	55·3	25·2
8	9·6	36·4	57·6	26·4	63·2	28·8
9	10·8	40·9	64	29·7	71·1	32·4
10	12	45·5	72	33	79	36
20	24	91	144	66	158	72
30	36	136	216	99	237	108
40	48	182	288	132	316	144
50	60	228	360	165	395	180
60	72	272	432	198	474	216
70	84	318	504	231	553	252
80	96	364	576	264	632	288
90	108	409	648	297	711	324
100	120	455	720	330	790	360
110	132	500	792	363	869	396
120	144	544	864	396	948	432
130	156	591	936	429	1027	468
140	168	636	1008	462	1106	504
150	180	680	1080	495	1185	540
160	192	728	1152	528	1264	576
170	204	773	1224	561	1343	612
180	216	818	1296	594	1422	648
190	228	864	1368	627	1501	684
200	240	910	1440	660	1580	720
300	360	1360	2160	990	2370	1080
400	480	1820	2880	1320	3160	1440
500	600	2280	3600	1650	3950	1800

DISTANCE CONVERSION
Nautical Miles to Statute Miles and Kilometres

Nautical Miles	Statute Miles	Kilometres
1	1·15	1·85
2	2·3	3·71
3	3·46	5·56
4	4·61	7·41
5	5·76	9·27
6	6·91	11·12
7	8·06	12·97
8	9·21	14·83
9	10·36	16·68
10	11·52	18·53
20	23·03	37·06
30	34·55	55·60
40	46·06	74·12
50	57·58	92·66
60	69·10	111·19
70	80·61	129·72
80	92·13	148·26
90	103·46	166·79
100	115·2	185·32
200	230·4	370·64
300	345·5	555·96
400	460·6	741·28
500	575·8	926·60
600	691·0	1111·92
700	806·1	1297·24
800	921·3	1482·56
900	1036·4	1667·88
1000	1151·6	1853·2

DISTANCE CONVERSION
Kilometres to Nautical Miles and Statute Miles

Kilometres	Nautical Miles	Statute Miles
1	0·54	0·62
2	1·08	1·24
3	1·62	1·86
4	2·16	2·49
5	2·70	3·11
6	3·24	3·73
7	3·78	4·35
8	4·32	4·97
9	4·86	5·59
10	5·40	6·21
20	10·79	12·43
30	16·19	18·64
40	21·58	24·86
50	26·98	31·07
60	32·38	37·28
70	37·77	43·50
80	43·17	49·71
90	48·56	55·93
100	53·96	62·14
200	107·92	124·28
300	161·88	186·42
400	215·84	248·56
500	269·80	310·70
600	323·76	372·84
700	377·72	434·98
800	431·68	497·12
900	485·64	559·26
1000	539·6	621·40

DISTANCE CONVERSION
Statute Miles to Nautical Miles and Kilometres

Statute Miles	Nautical Miles	Kilometres
1	0·87	1·61
2	1·74	3·22
3	2·61	4·83
4	3·47	6·44
5	4·34	8·05
6	5·21	9·66
7	6·08	11·27
8	6·95	12·88
9	7·82	14·49
10	8·68	16·09
20	17·37	32·19
30	26·05	48·28
40	34·74	64·38
50	43·42	80·47
60	51·10	96·56
70	60·79	112·66
80	69·47	128·75
90	78·16	144·85
100	86·84	160·94
200	173·7	321·88
300	260·5	482·82
400	347·4	643·76
500	434·2	804·70
600	521·0	965·64
700	607·9	1126·6
800	694·7	1287·5
900	781·6	1488·5
1000	868·4	1609·4

ALTITUDE CONVERSION

Feet (ft.) to Metres (m.)

ft.	m.	ft.	m.	ft.	m.	ft.	m.
1..	0·30	43..	13·11	85..	25·91	10,000..	3,048·0
2..	0·61	44..	13·41	86..	26·21	10,500..	3,200·4
3..	0·91	45..	13·72	87..	26·52	11,000..	3,352·8
4..	1·22	46..	14·02	88..	26·82	11,500..	3,505·2
5..	1·52	47..	14·33	89..	27·13	12,000..	3,657·6
6..	1·83	48..	14·63	90..	27·43	12,500..	3,810·0
7..	2·13	49..	14·94	91..	27·74	13,000..	3,962·4
8..	2·44	50..	15·24	92..	28·04	13,500..	4,114·8
9..	2·74	51..	15·54	93..	28·35	14,000..	4,267·2
10..	3·05	52..	15·85	94..	28·65	14,500..	4,419·6
11..	3·35	53..	16·15	95..	28·96	15,000..	4,572·0
12..	3·66	54..	16·46	96..	29·26	15,500..	4,724·4
13..	3·96	55..	16·76	97...	29·57	16,000..	4,876·8
14..	4·27	56..	17·07	98..	29·87	16,500..	5,029·2
15..	4·57	57..	17·37	99..	30·18	17,000..	5,181·6
16..	4·88	58..	17·68	100..	30·48	17,500..	5,334·0
17..	5·18	59..	17·98	200..	60·96	18,000..	5,486·4
18..	5·49	60..	18·29	300..	91·44	18,500..	5,638·8
19..	5·79	61..	18·59	400..	121·92	19,000..	5,791·2
20..	6·10	62..	18·90	500..	152·40	19,500..	5,943·6
21..	6·40	63..	19·20	600..	182·88	20,000..	6,096·0
22..	6·71	64..	19·51	700..	213·36	20,500..	6,248·4
23..	7·01	65..	19·81	800..	243·84	21,000..	6,400·8
24..	7·32	66..	20·12	900..	274·32	21,500..	6,553·2
25..	7·62	67..	20·42	1,000..	304·80	22,000..	6,705·6
26..	7·92	68..	20·73	1,500..	457·2	22,500..	6,858·0
27..	8·23	69..	21·03	2,000..	609·6	23,000..	7,010·4
28..	8·53	70..	21·34	2,500..	762·0	23,500..	7,162·8
29..	8·84	71..	21·64	3,000..	914·4	24,000..	7,315·2
30..	9·14	72..	21·95	3,500..	1,066·8	24,500..	7,467·6
31..	9·45	73..	22·25	4,000..	1,219·2	25,000..	7,620·0
32..	9·75	74..	22·56	4,500..	1,371·6	25,500..	7,772·4
33..	10·06	75..	22·86	5,000..	1,524·0	26,000..	7,924·8
34..	10·36	76..	23·16	5,500..	1,676·4	26,500..	8,077·2
35..	10·67	77..	23·47	6,000..	1,828·8	27,000..	8,229·6
36..	10·97	78..	23·77	6,500..	1,981·2	27,500..	8,382·0
37..	11·28	79..	24·08	7,000..	2,133·6	28,000..	8,534·4
38..	11·58	80..	24·38	7,500..	2,286·0	28,500..	8,686·8
39..	11·89	81..	24·69	8,000..	2,438·4	29,000..	8,839·2
40..	12·19	82..	24·99	8,500..	2,590·8	29,500..	8,991·6
41..	12·50	83..	25·30	9,000..	2,743·2	30,000..	9,144·0
42..	12·80	84..	25·60	9,500..	2,895·6		

ALTITUDE CONVERSION

Metres (m.) to Feet (ft.)

m.	ft.	m.	ft.	m.	ft.	m.	ft.
1..	3·28	43..141·08		85..	278·86	2,800..	9,186·3
2..	6·56	44..144·36		86..	282·15	2,900..	9,514·4
3..	9·84	45..147·64		87..	285·43	3,000..	9,842·5
4..	13·12	46..150·92		88..	288·71	3,100..10,170·6	
5..	16·41	47..154·20		89..	291·99	3,200..10,498·7	
6..	19·68	48..157·48		90..	295·27	3,300..10,826·7	
7..	22·97	49..160·76		91..	298·56	3,400..11,154·8	
8..	26·25	50..164·04		92..	301·84	3,500..11,482·9	
9..	29·53	51..167·32		93..	305·12	3,600..11,811·0	
10..	32·81	52..170·60		94..	308·40	3,700..12,139·1	
11..	36·09	53..173·88		95..	311·68	3,800..12,467·2	
12..	39·37	54..177·16		96..	314·96	3,900..12,795·2	
13..	42·65	55..180·45		97..	318·24	4,000..13,123·3	
14..	45·93	56..183·73		98..	321·52	4,100..13,451·4	
15..	49·21	57..187·01		99..	324·80	4,200..13,779·5	
16..	52·49	58..190·29		100..	328·08	4,300..14,107·6	
17..	55·77	59..193·57		200..	656·2	4,400..14,435·7	
18..	59·05	60..196·85		300..	984·3	4,500..14,763·7	
19..	62·34	61..200·13		400..1,312·3		4,600..15,091·8	
20..	65·62	62..203·41		500..1,640·4		4,700..15,419·9	
21..	68·90	63..206·69		600..1,968·5		4,800..15,748·0	
22..	72·18	64..209·97		700..2,296·6		4,900..16,076·1	
23..	75·46	65..213·25		800..2,624·7		5,000..16,404·2	
24..	78·74	66..216·53		900..2,952·7		5,100..16,732·2	
25..	82·02	67..219·82		1,000..3,280·8		5,200..17,060·3	
26..	85·30	68..223·10		1,100..3,608·9		5,300..17,388·4	
27..	88·58	69..226·38		1,200..3,937·0		5,400..17,716·5	
28..	91·86	70..229·66		1,300..4,265·1		5,500..18,044·6	
29..	95·14	71..232·94		1,400..4,593·2		5,600..18,372·7	
30..	98·42	72..236·22		1,500..4,921·2		5,700..18,700·7	
31..101·71		73..239·50		1,600..5,249·3		5,800..19,028·8	
32..104·99		74..242·78		1,700..5,577·4		5,900..19,356·9	
33..108·27		75..246·06		1,800..5,905·5		6,000..19,685·0	
34..111·55		76..249·34		1,900..6,233·6		6,100..20,013·1	
35..114·83		77..252·62		2,000..6,561·7		6,200..20,341·2	
36..118·11		78..255·90		2,100..6,889·7		6,300..20,669·2	
37..121·39		79..259·19		2,200..7,217·8		6,400..20,997·3	
38..124·67		80..262·47		2,300..7,545·9		6,500..21,325·4	
39..127·95		81..265·75		2,400..7,874·0		7,000..22,965·8	
40..131·23		82..269·03		2,500..8,202·1		8,000..26,246·7	
41..134·51		83..272·31		2,600..8,530·2		9,000..29,527·5	
42..137·79		84..275·59		2,700..8,858·2		10,000..32,808·4	

Conversion Tables

WEIGHT CONVERSION

Pounds (lb.) to Kilograms (kg.)

lb.	kg.	lb.	kg.	lb.	kg.
1 ..	0·45	41 ..	18·60	81 ..	36·74
2 ..	0·91	42 ..	19·05	82 ..	37·20
3 ..	1·36	43 ..	19·51	83 ..	37·65
4 ..	1·81	44 ..	19·96	84 ..	38·10
5 ..	2·27	45 ..	20·41	85 ..	39·56
6 ..	2·72	46 ..	20·87	86 ..	39·01
7 ..	3·18	47 ..	21·32	87 ..	38·46
8 ..	3·63	48 ..	21·77	88 ..	39·92
9 ..	4·08	49 ..	22·23	89 ..	40·37
10 ..	4·54	50 ..	22·68	90 ..	40·82
11 ..	4·99	51 ..	23·13	91 ..	41·28
12 ..	5·44	52 ..	23·59	92 ..	41·73
13 ..	5·90	53 ..	24·04	93 ..	42·19
14 ..	6·35	54 ..	24·49	94 ..	42·64
15 ..	6·80	55 ..	24·95	95 ..	43·09
16 ..	7·26	56 ..	25·40	96 ..	43·55
17 ..	7·71	57 ..	25·86	97 ..	44·00
18 ..	8·17	58 ..	26·31	98 ..	44·45
19 ..	8·62	59 ..	26·76	99 ..	44·91
20 ..	9·07	60 ..	27·22	100 ..	45·4
21 ..	9·53	61 ..	27·67	112 ..	50·8
22 ..	9·98	62 ..	28·12	200 ..	90·7
23 ..	10·43	63 ..	28·58	300 ..	136·1
24 ..	10·89	64 ..	29·03	400 ..	181·4
25 ..	11·34	65 ..	29·48	500 ..	226·8
26 ..	11·79	66 ..	29·94	600 ..	272·2
27 ..	12·25	67 ..	30·39	700 ..	317·5
28 ..	12·70	68 ..	30·84	800 ..	362·9
29 ..	13·15	69 ..	31·30	900 ..	408·2
30 ..	13·61	70 ..	31·75	1,000 ..	453·6
31 ..	14·06	71 ..	32·31	2,000 ..	907·2
32 ..	14·52	72 ..	32·66	2,240 ..	1,016·1
33 ..	14·97	73 ..	33·11	3,000 ..	1,360·8
34 ..	15·42	74 ..	33·57	4,000 ..	1,814·4
35 ..	15·88	75 ..	34·02	5,000 ..	2,268·0
36 ..	16·33	76 ..	34·47	6,000 ..	2,721·6
37 ..	16·78	77 ..	34·93	7,000 ..	3,175·2
38 ..	17·24	78 ..	35·38	8,000 ..	3,628·8
39 ..	17·69	79 ..	35·83	9,000 ..	4,082·4
40 ..	18·14	80 ..	36·29	10,000 ..	4,536·0

14 lb. = 1 stone
2,000 lb. = 1 short ton

112 lb. = 1 hundredweight (cwt.)
2,240 lb. = 1 long ton

WEIGHT CONVERSION

Kilograms (kg.) to Pounds (lb.)

kg.	lb.	kg.	lb.	kg.	lb.
1 ..	2·20	41 ..	90·39	81 ..	178·57
2 ..	4·41	42 ..	92·59	82 ..	180·78
3 ..	6·61	43 ..	94·80	83 ..	182·98
4 ..	8·82	44 ..	97·00	84 ..	185·19
5 ..	11·02	45 ..	99·21	85 ..	187·39
6 ..	13·23	46 ..	101·41	86 ..	189·60
7 ..	15·43	47 ..	103·62	87 ..	191·80
8 ..	17·64	48 ..	105·82	88 ..	194·01
9 ..	19·84	49 ..	108·03	89 ..	196·21
10 ..	22·05	50 ..	110·23	90 ..	198·41
11 ..	24·25	51 ..	112·44	91 ..	200·62
12 ..	26·46	52 ..	114·64	92 ..	202·82
13 ..	28·66	53 ..	116·84	93 ..	205·03
14 ..	30·86	54 ..	119·05	94 ..	207·23
15 ..	33·07	55 ..	121·25	95 ..	209·44
16 ..	35·27	56 ..	123·46	96 ..	211·64
17 ..	37·48	57 ..	125·66	97 ..	213·85
18 ..	39·68	58 ..	127·87	98 ..	216·05
19 ..	41·89	59 ..	130·07	99 ..	218·26
20 ..	44·09	60 ..	132·28	100 ..	220·5
21 ..	46·30	61 ..	134·48	200 ..	440·9
22 ..	48·50	62 ..	136·69	300 ..	661·4
23 ..	50·71	63 ..	138·89	400 ..	881·8
24 ..	50·91	64 ..	141·09	500 ..	1,102·3
25 ..	55·12	65 ..	143·30	600 ..	1,322·8
26 ..	57·32	66 ..	145·60	700 ..	1,543·2
27 ..	59·52	67 ..	147·71	800 ..	1,763·7
28 ..	61·73	68 ..	149·91	900 ..	1,984·1
29 ..	63·93	69 ..	152·12	1,000 ..	2,204·6
30 ..	66·14	70 ..	154·32	2,000 ..	4,409·2
31 ..	68·34	71 ..	156·53	3,000 ..	6,613·8
32 ..	70·55	72 ..	158·73	4,000 ..	8·818·4
33 ..	72·75	73 ..	160·94	5,000 ..	11,023·0
34 ..	74·96	74 ..	163·14	6,000 ..	13,227·6
35 ..	77·16	75 ..	165·35	7,000 ..	15,432·2
36 ..	79·37	76 ..	166·55	8,000 ..	17,636·8
37 ..	81·57	77 ..	169·75	9,000 ..	19,841·4
38 ..	83·78	78 ..	171·96	10,000 ..	22,046·0
39 ..	85·98	79 ..	174·16		
40 ..	88·18	80 ..	176·37		

1,000 kg. = 1 Metric Ton

BAROMETRIC PRESSURE CONVERSION

Inches	Millibars	Inches	Millibars	Inches	Millibars
28·00 ..	948·2	28·50 ..	965·1	29·00 ..	982·1
28·01 ..	948·5	28·51 ..	965·5	29·01 ..	982·4
28·02 ..	948·9	28·52 ..	965·8	29·02 ..	982·7
28·03 ..	949·2	28·53 ..	966·1	29·03 ..	983·1
28·04 ..	949·5	28·54 ..	866·5	29·04 ..	983·4
28·05 ..	949·9	28·55 ..	966·8	29·05 ..	983·7
28·06 ..	950·2	28·56 ..	967·2	29·06 ..	984·1
28·07 ..	950·6	28·57 ..	967·5	29·07 ..	984·4
28·08 ..	950·9	28·58 ..	967·8	29·08 ..	984·8
28·09 ..	951·2	28·59 ..	968·2	29·09 ..	985·1
28·10 ..	951·6	28·60 ..	968·5	29·10 ..	985·4
28·11 ..	951·9	28·61 ..	968·8	29·11 ..	985·8
28·12 ..	952·3	28·62 ..	969·2	29·12 ..	986·1
28·13 ..	952·6	28·63 ..	969·5	29 13 ..	986·5
28·14 ..	952·9	28·64 ..	969·9	29·14 ..	986·8
28·15 ..	953·3	28·65 ..	970·2	29·15 ..	987·1
28·16 ..	953·6	28·66 ..	970·5	29·16 ..	987·5
28·17 ..	953·9	28·67 ..	970·9	29·17 ..	987·8
28·18 ..	954·3	28·68 ..	971·2	29·18 ..	988·2
28·19 ..	954·6	28·69 ..	971·6	29·19 ..	988·5
28·20 ..	955·0	28·70 ..	971·9	29·20 ..	988·8
28·21 ..	955·3	28·71 ..	972·2	29·21 ..	989·2
28·22 ..	955·6	28·72 ..	972·6	29·22 ..	989·5
28·23 ..	956·0	28·73 ..	972·9	29·23 ..	989·8
28·24 ..	956 3	28·74 ..	973·2	29·24 ..	990·2
28·25 ..	956·7	28·75 ..	973·6	29·25 ..	990·5
28·26 ..	957·0	28·76 ..	973·9	29·26 ..	990·9
28·27 ..	957·3	28·77 ..	974·3	29·27 ..	991·2
28·28 ..	957·7	28·78 ..	974·6	29·28 ..	991·5
28·29 ..	958·0	28·79 ..	974·9	29·29 ..	991·9
28·30 ..	958·3	28·80 ..	975·3	29·30 ..	992·2
28·31 ..	958·7	28·81 ..	975·6	29·31 ..	992·6
28·32 ..	959·0	28·82 ..	976·0	29·32 ..	992·9
28·33 ..	959·4	28·83 ..	976·3	29·33 ..	993·2
28·34 ..	959·7	28·84 ..	976·6	29·34 ..	993·6
28·35 ..	960·0	28·85 ..	977·0	29·35 ..	993·9
28·36 ..	960·4	28·86 ..	977·3	29·36 ..	994·2
28·37 ..	960·7	28·87 ..	977·7	29·37 ..	994·6
28·38 ..	961·1	28·88 ..	978·0	29·38 ..	994·9
28·39 ..	961·4	28·89 ..	978·3	29·39 ..	995·3
28·40 ..	961·7	28·90 ..	978·7	29·40 ..	995·6
28·41 ..	962·1	28·91 ..	979·0	29·41 ..	995·9
28·42 ..	962·4	28·92 ..	979·3	29·42 ..	996·3
28·43 ..	962·8	28·93 ..	979·7	29·43 ..	996·6
28·44 ..	963·1	28·94 ..	980·0	29·44 ..	997·0
29·45 ..	963·4	28·95 ..	980·4	29·45 ..	997·3
28·46 ..	963·8	28·96 ..	980·7	29·46 ..	997·6
28·47 ..	964·1	28·97 ..	981·0	29·47 ..	998·0
28·48 ..	964·4	28·98 ..	981·4	29·48 ..	998·3
28·49 ..	964·8	28·99 ..	981·7	29·49 ..	998·6

BAROMETRIC PRESSURE CONVERSION

Inches	Millibars	Inches	Millibars	Inches	Millibars
29·50 ..	999·0	30·00 ..	1,015·9	30·50 ..	1,032·9
29·51 ..	999·3	30·01 ..	1,016·3	30·51 ..	1,033·2
29·52 ..	999·7	30·02 ..	1,016·6	30·52 ..	1,033·5
29·53 ..	1,000·0	30·03 ..	1,016·9	30·53 ..	1,033·9
29·54 ..	1,000·4	30·04 ..	1,017·3	30·54 ..	1,034·2
29·55 ..	1,000·7	30·05 ..	1,017·6	30·55 ..	1,034·5
29·56 ..	1,001·0	30·06 ..	1,018·0	30·56 ..	1,034·9
29·57 ..	1,001·4	30·07 ..	1,018·3	30·57 ..	1,035·2
29·58 ..	1,001·7	30·08 ..	1,018·6	30·58 ..	1,035·5
29·59 ..	1,002·0	30·09 ..	1,019·0	30·59 ..	1,035·9
29·60 ..	1,002·4	30·10 ..	1,019·3	30·60 ..	1,036·2
29·61 ..	1,002·7	30·11 ..	1,019·6	30·61 ..	1,036·6
29·62 ..	1,003·1	30·12 ..	1,020·0	30·62 ..	1,036·9
29·63 ..	1,003·4	30·13 ..	1,020·3	30·63 ..	1,037·3
29·64 ..	1,003·7	30·14 ..	1,020·7	30·64 ..	1,037·6
29·65 ..	1,004·1	30·15 ..	1,021·0	30·65 ..	1,037·9
29·66 ..	1,004·4	30·16 ..	1,021·3	30·66 ..	1,038·3
29·67 ..	1,004·7	30·17 ..	1,021·7	30·67 ..	1,038·6
29·68 ..	1,005·1	30·18 ..	1,022·0	30·68 ..	1,038·9
29·69 ..	1,005·4	30·19 ..	1,022·4	30·69 ..	1,039·3
29·70 ..	1,005·8	30·20 ..	1,022·7	30·70 ..	1,039·6
29·71 ..	1,006·1	30·21 ..	1,023·0	30·71 ..	1,040·0
29·72 ..	1,006·4	30·22 ..	1,023·4	30·72 ..	1,040·3
29·73 ..	1,006·8	30·23 ..	1,023·7	30·73 ..	1,040·6
29·74 ..	1,007·1	30·24 ..	1,024·0	30·74 ..	1,041·0
29·75 ..	1,007·5	30·25 ..	1,024·4	30·75 ..	1,041·3
29·76 ..	1,007·8	30·26 ..	1,024·7	30·76 ..	1,041·7
29·77 ..	1,008·1	30·27 ..	1,025·1	30·77 ..	1,042·0
29·78 ..	1,008·5	30·28 ..	1,025·4	30·78 ..	1,042·3
29·79 ..	1,008·8	30·29 ..	1,025·7	30·79 ..	1,042·7
29·80 ..	1,009·1	30·30 ..	1,026·1	30·80 ..	1,043·0
29·81 ..	1,009·5	30·31 ..	1,026·4	30·81 ..	1,043·3
29·82 ..	1,009·8	30·32 ..	1,026·7	30·82 ..	1,043·7
29·83 ..	1,010·2	30·33 ..	1,027·1	30·83 ..	1,044·0
29·84 ..	1,010·5	30·34 ..	1,027·4	30·84 ..	1,044·4
29·85 ..	1,010·8	30·35 ..	1,027·8	30·85 ..	1,044·7
29·86 ..	1,011·2	30·36 ..	1,028·1	30·86 ..	1,045·0
29·87 ..	1,011·5	30·37 ..	1,028·4	30·87 ..	1,045·4
29·88 ..	1,011·9	30·38 ..	1,028·8	30·88 ..	1,045·7
29·89 ..	1,012·2	30·39 ..	1,029·1	30·89 ..	1,046·1
29·90 ..	1,012·5	30·40 ..	1,029·5	30·90 ..	1,046·4
29·91 ..	1,012·9	30·41 ..	1,029·8	30·91 ..	1,046·7
29·92 ..	1,013·2	30·42 ..	1,030·1	30·92 ..	1,047·1
29·93 ..	1,013·5	30·43 ..	1,030·5	30·93 ..	1,047·4
29·94 ..	1,013·9	30·44 ..	1,030·8	30·94 ..	1,047·8
29·95 ..	1,914·2	30·45 ..	1,031·2	30·95 ..	1,048·1
29·96 ..	1,014·6	30·46 ..	1,031·5	30·96 ..	1,048·4
29·97 ..	1,014·9	30·47 ..	1,031·8	30·97 ..	1,048·8
29·98 ..	1,015·2	30·48 ..	1,032·2	30·98 ..	1,049·1
29·99 ..	1,015·6	30·49 ..	1,032·5	30·99 ..	1,049·5

WIND COMPONENT TABLES
CROSSWIND

ANGLE BETWEEN WIND DIRECTION AND RUNWAY HEADING

		10°	20°	30°	40°	50°	60°	70°	80°
W I N D S P E E D	5	1	2	2	3	4	4	4	5
	10	2	3	5	6	7	8	9	9
	15	3	5	7	9	11	13	14	14
	20	3	7	10	13	15	17	18	19
	25	4	8	12	16	19	22	23	24
	30	5	10	15	19	23	26	28	29
K N O T S	35	6	12	17	22	26	30	32	34
	40	7	14	20	25	30	35	37	39
	45	8	15	22	29	34	39	42	44
	50	9	17	25	32	38	43	47	49

HEADWIND

ANGLE BETWEEN WIND DIRECTION AND RUNWAY HEADING

		10°	20°	30°	40°	50°	60°	70°	80°
W I N D S P E E D	5	5	4	4	4	3	2	2	1
	10	9	9	8	7	6	5	3	2
	15	14	14	13	11	9	7	5	3
	20	19	18	17	15	13	10	7	3
	25	24	23	22	19	16	12	8	4
	30	29	28	26	23	19	15	10	5
K N O T S	35	34	32	30	26	22	17	12	6
	40	39	37	35	30	25	20	14	7
	45	44	42	39	34	29	22	15	8
	50	49	47	43	38	32	25	17	9

DME AND TACAN
FREQUENCY/CHANNEL PAIRING TABLES

X CHANNELS

MHz	·00	·10	·20	·30	·40	·50	·60	·70	·80	·90
108	17	18	19	20	21	22	23	24	25	26
109	27	28	29	30	31	32	33	34	35	36
110	37	38	39	40	41	42	43	44	45	46
111	47	48	49	50	51	52	53	54	55	56
112	57	58	59	70	71	72	73	74	75	76
113	77	78	79	80	81	82	83	84	85	86
114	87	88	89	90	91	92	93	94	95	96
115	97	98	99	100	101	102	103	104	105	106
116	107	108	109	110	111	112	113	114	115	116
117	117	118	119	120	121	122	123	124	125	126
133	—	—	—	60	61	62	63	64	65	66
134	67	68	69	—	1	2	3	4	5	6
135	7	8	9	10	11	12	13	14	15	16

Y CHANNELS

MHz	·05	·15	·25	·35	·45	·55	·65	·75	·85	·95
108	17	18	19	20	21	22	23	24	25	26
109	27	28	29	30	31	32	33	34	35	36
110	37	38	39	40	41	42	43	44	45	46
111	47	48	49	50	51	52	53	54	55	56
112	57	58	59	70	71	72	73	74	75	76
113	77	78	79	80	81	82	83	84	85	86
114	87	88	89	90	91	92	93	94	95	96
115	97	98	99	100	101	102	103	104	105	106
116	107	108	109	110	111	112	113	114	115	116
117	117	118	119	120	121	122	123	124	125	126

Intentionally Blank

ABBREVIATIONS

AAL.........Above Aerodrome Level
A.Bn........Aerodrome Beacon
ACC........Area Control Centre
A/C.........Aircraft
A/D.........Aerodrome
AFIS.......Aerodrome Flight Information
          Service
AFTN......Aeronautical Fixed
          Telecommunications Network
A/G.........Air/Ground communication station
AGL........Above Ground Level
AIS.........Aeronautical Information Service
ALT.........Altitude
AMSL......Above Mean Sea Level
Ap..........Approach (Lighting)
App........Approach
APP........Approach Control
ARP........Aerodrome Reference Point
ATC........Air Traffic Control
ATCC......Air Traffic Control Centre
ATIS   Automatic Terminal Information
          Service
ATS........Air Traffic Service
Awy........Airway
BMSL.....Below Mean Sea Level
c/s..........Callsign
CTA........Control Area
CTR........Control Zone
DME.......Distance Measuring Equipment
DVOR.....Doppler VOR
E.............East
Elev........Elevation
ETA........Estimated Time of Arrival
ETD........Estimated Time of Departure
FIC.........Flight Information Centre
FIR.........Flight Information Region
FIS.........Flight Information Service
FL...........Flight Level
freq........Frequency
ft.............Feet
GND.......Ground Control
Gn..........Green
H24.........Continuous Operation
HEL........Helicopter
HF.........High Frequency
HJ...........Sunrise to Sunset
HN..........Sunset to Sunrise
HO..........Hours for operational requirements
HX..........No specific operating hours
I.Bcn.......Ident Beacon
ICAO.......Intl. Civil Aviation Organisation

IFR.........Instrument Flight Rules
ILS..........Instrument Landing System
IMC.........Instrument Meteorological
          Conditions
Kg...........Kilogram
Km..........Kilometre
Kts..........Knots
lbs...........Pounds
LLZ.........Localiser
Lctr.........Locator (NDB)
M.............Magnetic
Met.........Meteorological Facility
MIL..........Military
MTWA.....Maximum Total Weight Authorised
N..............North
NDB........Non-directional Radio Beacon
nm...........Nautical Miles
O/R..........On Request
O/T.........Other times
P.............Primary (frequency)
PAPI........Precision Approach Path Indicator
PNR........Prior Notification Required
PPR........Prior Permission Required
R.............Red. Radial (VOR)
RAD.......Radar
RCL........Runway Centreline Lighting
Rwy........Runway
R/T.........Radio Telephony
S.............South
SAR........Search and Rescue
SR..........Sunrise
SS..........Sunset
SWL.......Single Wheel Load
TACAN....Tactical Air Navigation Equipment
Tel..........Telephone
Thr..........Threshold
TMA.......Terminal Control Area
TVOR......Terminal VOR (low power)
TWR.......Tower Control
VAD........Visual Approach/Departure
VASIS.....Visual Approach Slope Indicator
VDF........VHF Direction Finding
VFR........Visual Flight Rules
VHF........Very High Frequency
VMC.......Visual Meteorological Conditions
VOR........VHF Omni-directional Radio Range
VORTAC..VOR & TACAN (co-located)
VOT........VOR Receiver Test facility
W.............West
Wh...........White

PHONETIC ALPHABET
AND
MORSE CODE

A.....Alpha .... • —
B.....Bravo .... — • • •
C.....Charlie .... — • — •
D.....Delta................. — • •
E.....Echo................. •
F.....Foxtrot .... • • — •
G.....Golf .... — — •
H.....Hotel .... • • • •
I......India .... • •
J.....Juliet .... • — — —
K.....Kilo.................. — • —
L.....Lima .... • — • •
M....Mike .... — —
N.....November ...... — •
O.....Oscar .... — — —
P.....Papa................. • — — •
Q.....Quebec .... — — • —
R.....Romeo .... • — •
S.....Sierra .... • • •
T.....Tango.............. —
U.....Uniform........... • • —
V.....Victor .... • • • —
W....Whisky............ • — —
X.....X-ray............... — • • —
Y.....Yankee .... — • — —
Z.....Zulu .... — — • •